1982

University of St. Francis
GEN   822.33 O2c

S0-BRL-481

3 0301 00089485

The *All's Well* Story

THE *All's Well* STORY FROM
BOCCACCIO TO SHAKESPEARE

Howard C. Cole

UNIVERSITY OF ILLINOIS PRESS

Urbana   Chicago   London

LIBRARY
College of St. Francis
JOLIET, ILL.

*Publication of this work has been made possible in part
by a grant from the Andrew W. Mellon Foundation.*

© 1981 by the Board of Trustees of the University of Illinois
Manufactured in the United States of America

Library of Congress Cataloging in Publication Data

Cole, Howard C.
  The All's Well Story from Boccaccio to Shakespeare.

  Bibliography: p. 139.
  1. Shakespeare, William, 1564-1616. All's well
that ends well. 2. Shakespeare, William, 1564-
1616. All's well that ends well—Sources.
3. Boccaccio, Giovanni, 1313-1375. Decamerone.
4. Boccaccio, Giovanni, 1313-1375—Influence.
I. Title
PR2801.C6   822.3'3   81-2474
ISBN 0-252-00883-9   AACR2

822.33
O2c

For Mine Owne Dear Clever Wenches:
Bunny,
Kris &
Sonie

102634

Contents

Preface

The consideration of this made Mr. Hales of Eton
say that there was no subject of which any poet ever
writ, but he would produce it much better treated of
in Shakespeare.

John Dryden, *An Essay of Dramatic Poesy*

The hero of this study is not Shakespeare, much less
Boccaccio, but the "coming-forthness" of a story they both told, an
account of the remarkably different uses to which writers of several
centuries put one of the *Decameron*'s simplest tales. My orientation is
admittedly as Shakespearean as John Hales's: interest in the *All's Well*
story was inspired by its best known chapter, and a comparative reading
of the play has been my constant goal, regardless of occasional "digres-
sions." I have continually resisted, however, a method often employed
in essays of this kind, that of treating each precursor merely as a source,
of dealing only with what Shakespeare made of him and consequently
ignoring whatever else he may have been attempting. We should be able
to make better sense of the play once we understand its story, but to
understand the story we must seek to render intelligible the designs of
every contributor, whether or not we can determine which designs
Shakespeare borrowed from, thoughtfully rejected, or utterly failed to
grasp.

Setting the story to rights, then, involves temporarily suspending
our knowledge of the consequences, measuring each writer not against
a future he unknowingly helped to shape but against a past he consciously worked with and a present whose influences he could not
escape. What may at first appear a digression (Burgundian politics of
the 1470s, for example, or the cynicism of Leo X's jaded versifiers)

merits—indeed, *requires*—consideration if it eventually aids us in seeing any part of the whole more clearly. Similarly, we must never assume that the writer's knowledge of the tradition he essayed was based only upon his immediate predecessors. It is highly unlikely, for instance, that Shakespeare knew all eight sixteenth-century Italian and French editions of the *Decameron* listed in the Selective Bibliography, but it is just as unlikely that he knew no more than what he found in Painter's translations. In re-creating all possible avenues of creative imitation as they might have appeared to each contributor, we cannot afford to overlook the humblest springboard for his imagination, however distanced by time or place. Finally, whereas different parts of this study are bound to interest different readers—the Italian specialist, the Shakespearean, the student of comparative literature—it is hoped that, after surveying the evidence, all parties will agree that the *All's Well* story is far more complex than hitherto imagined, that Geoffrey Bullough is wrong on both counts when he claims that "Shakespeare has taken a fairy-tale and made of it a morality."

Given this book's mixed audience, several remarks on method also seem in order. First, in discussing Continental works I have tried to select as illustrative and supportive passages those which require only an elementary knowledge of French and Italian. In Chapter II, where I cannot avoid a close reading of the *Decameron*'s Third Day, citations are to a modern English translation, but all have been checked against Vittore Branca's two-volume edition and any significant differences are noted. In Chapter IV, on the other hand, where Bernardo Accolti's borrowings from Boccaccio are examined and the *Decameron* must be cited in Italian, I have partly paraphrased both authors within the discussion. Secondly, aside from normalizing *u, v,* and long *s,* I have not emended the texts of the *Virginia* and *Le Chevalereux Comte d'Artois*. Students of Italian will no more be misled by Accolti without accent marks (e.g., "gia," "cosi") than Shakespeareans by Painter's "condempned to . . . prison" or Florio's "bene published before." Genuinely misleading words, however, are followed by bracketed queries (e.g., the French romance's "conculd [conclut?]"). Third, whereas any index beyond the outline of the Contents seemed unnecessary, I have provided a bibliography that includes chronological listings of those editions of Boccaccio and Shakespeare which have proved especially helpful. Here, of course, the reader will also find complete bibliographical descriptions of all the works cited in the notes.

In ranging so far from my original goal, a study of Shakespeare's development as a comic craftsman, I have incurred numerous obligations. Gwynne Evans and Robert Ornstein offered advice and encouragement at an early and crucial stage. I also wish to thank Gabriel Savignon and Marie Schwacke for guiding me through several difficult passages of French and German respectively. To Angelina Pietrangeli I owe a greater debt, nothing less than bringing my GI Italian up to Accolti's level and then rescuing me from a few serious misreadings. I appreciate as well the generosity of the editors of *Modern Language Notes* and *Renaissance Drama* for accepting earlier versions of Chapters II and IV respectively and allowing them to be used here. I am also grateful to the departmental secretaries, Marlyn Ehlers and Rene Wahlfeldt, who must have dreaded typing so much foreign stuff but never complained. My greatest obligation, though, is to my wife and daughters, who sacrificed vacations to this project and were more confident than I that it would someday be completed. To them it is most affectionately dedicated.

Howard C. Cole
Champaign, Illinois
January, 1981

I

Preliminary Concerns:
Tradition and Innovation
in the *All's Well* Story

It is clear that, from the point of view of narrative traditions still accepted in Shakespeare's day, the conduct of Helena in fulfilling the conditions set by Bertram for their union was admirable . . . and that the "happy ending" was accepted as a convention of drama because it was also a convention of story-telling.

W. W. Lawrence, *Shakespeare's Problem Comedies*

No Shakespearean play has elicited so many disparate responses as *All's Well That Ends Well*. Since the early eighteenth century this perplexing work has been read and staged as farcical comedy, sentimental romance, serious drama, romantic fable, cynical satire, and thematic-symbolic dramatization.[1] Given the play's elusive mood and tone, it is not surprising to find its heroine snarled at by Mrs. Lennox and gushed over by Mrs. Jameson, subordinated in Garrick's production and highlighted in Kemble's. What is surprising, however, is that more recent and presumably more scholarly interpreters have been just as subjective in selecting the backgrounds that best support their radically different views. Helena, in short, now approaches divinity (or nymphomania), trailing clouds of footnotes.

The most detailed and probably the most influential historical criticism of *All's Well* stems from W. W. Lawrence's attempts to objectify Helena as a medieval stereotype, the Clever Wench, and to relate the play's main plot to two conventional folk motifs, "The Fulfilment

of the Tasks" and "The Healing of the King."[2] The more analogues
Lawrence advances to document the play's conventionality, however,
the more apparent the playwright's innovations become. The direct,
simple one-dimensional Virtue Story makes even clearer "the moral,
intellectual, and psychological depths which Shakespeare lent to his
source materials."[3] No truly Clever Wench would risk a world in which
ethical norms are repeatedly entertained—a world, as G. Wilson Knight
observes, "well saturated with religious thought and language."[4] But
if Lawrence's preoccupation with the tradition obscures Shakespeare's
contribution to it, Knight's customary theologizing leads to a different
oversimplification, the vision of Helena as "a redeeming power"
functioning "almost as Christ within the Christian Scheme."[5]

Some sort of oversimplification would seem unavoidable in tracing
a design as mingled as the "web of . . . life" it represents. Certainly
the most perceptive essays of the last few decades finally admit that if
the problems have become more clarified, they have not been fully
resolved,[6] and it is difficult to come away from Clifford Leech's
disarming catalogue of dramatic oddities[7] with the happy assurance
that Shakespeare was simply moralizing upon virtue as the true nobility
or, for that matter, that he was *simply* doing anything. "Lawrence's
basic interpretation of the play in terms of plot-material is just and
cannot be ignored," concludes G. K. Hunter, "but other elements . . .
complicate it out of recognition. Critical realism accompanies fairy-
tale, satire shadows spirituality, complex moral perceptions deny us
a simplicity of approach, complex intellectual interests demand an
analytical and detached attitude to the characters."[8] And if we cannot
make sense out of one part of the play without making nonsense out
of the others, we must admit that Shakespeare attempted too many
things to make all end well, that imagination flagged, leaving the effect
blurred and the fusion incomplete.[9]

Before allowing *All's Well*'s complexities to turn it into a complicated
failure, we should first notice that some difficulties have only been
compounded by the introduction of backgrounds of questionable
relevance. Having convinced us of the play's religious mood through
internal citation, for example, Knight finally deals with the passage
that inspired his essay's title, "The Third Eye," Helena's explanation
to the King of how her dying father "bade me store up, as a triple eye, /

Safer than mine own two, more dear" the most precious of his "many receipts."[10] This "choice secret," maintains Knight, "is the 'third eye' of occult doctrine and practice, located on the forehead and used in spirit-healing as a source of powerful rays."[11] At this point external evidence—several recent studies of the occult and *The Tibetan Book of the Dead*—is enlisted to illuminate the heroine's "mediumistic gifts."

But a far likelier source suggests a less exotic reading. We know that about the turn of the century Shakespeare was working on *Troilus and Cressida* and probably reading Speght's "newly Printed" folio edition of Chaucer. Only ten stanzas after describing Troilus sighing upon the Trojan walls—a vignette Lorenzo had already appropriated[12]— Chaucer pictures Criseyde lamenting that she lacked the prudence to steal away with her love:

> To late is now to speke of that matere
> Prudence alas, one of thine eien thre
> Me lacked alway, er that I came here
> For on time passed wel remembred me
> And present time eke could I wel se
> But future time, er I was in the snare
> Could I not sene, that causeth now my care.[13]

Just as Desdemona is told that her fate depends on that of her handker-chief—"Make it a darling like your precious eye" (*Oth.*, III. iv. 66)— Helena was bidden to treasure "th' only darling" of her father's "old experience." Each heroine's future happiness obviously hangs upon her foresight, Prudence's third and most precious eye. Knight's anachron-istic sources, on the other hand, only lead to an anachronistic gloss. The occult eye, moreover, blinds him to that satire shadowing spiritual-ity, the bawdy ushering in of Helena by Lafew, "Cressid's uncle."

The longest study of *All's Well*, Joseph Price's *The Unfortunate Comedy*, is usually more cautious in its use of backgrounds. The "historical framework" Price erects, however, consists of "an exhaus-tive theatrical and critical history to 1964,"[14] not the creative frame-work surrounding the playwright. It is only when Price finally turns from describing what was done to Shakespeare to interpreting what Shakespeare was really trying to do that he deals at least superficially with Elizabethan matters. Essential to his point that Bertram's refusal of Helena shows "contempt and error" opposing "love and right," for instance, is his prefatory claim, "that the King had the right to confer nobility upon Helena was a commonplace to the Elizabethans," followed by references to two historical studies.[15] But both studies complicate our response to this scene with other commonplaces Price ignores. The first notes that however frequently contemporary moral treatises insisted upon equating nobility with virtue, they did not fundamentally alter the class structure of the societies Shakespeare lived in and usually affirmed in his plays. If the audience did not question Helena's being entitled to "nobility dative," her rightfully gaining a title for services rendered to the state, it would surely wonder why the King's speech "emphasizes to an unusual degree the inportance of mere virtue."[16] The second study offers an extended history of how the rights of guardianship were abused—"Sometimes it has all the elements of a selfish and mercenary exploitation"—and includes Bertram among those noblemen who did not take direct action against their guardians for disparagement.[17] Unlike the background to which Knight appeals, Price's "commonplace" is relevant. But it is also incomplete and therefore temporarily muddies an otherwise perceptive essay in the new critical vein.

The most direct and frequent appeals to literary traditions are of course made by Lawrence, yet even he fails to take a complete survey of the materials available to Shakespeare. At the outset we are told that the main plot of *All's Well* comes from the ninth story of the Third Day of Boccaccio's *Decameron,* a tale that "Shakespeare in all probability got from the faithful translation in Painter's *Palace of Pleasure.*"[18] Immediately following this is an extensive explanatory note that first points out the unlikelihood of both Englishmen independently calling the people of Siena "the Senois," next mentions several attempts to show Shakespeare's dependence upon an Italian comedy based on Boccaccio, Bernardo Accolti's *Virginia* (acted in 1494), then cites other scholars who find the evidence unconvincing, and concludes by stating that "no further mention will be made of Accolti's play."[19] If Lawrence were dealing exclusively in fully documented, direct sources, we might understand Accolti's being sloughed off in a footnote. But immediately after summarizing Shakespeare's ultimate source, Lawrence begins outlining Oriental fairy tales and Scandinavian sagas "from which instructive conclusions may be drawn as to the general significance of the story as told by Boccaccio and by Shakespeare."[20] Even if Shakespeare had never heard of Accolti—and there are similarities between *All's Well* and *Virginia* much more striking than the one Lawrence uses to link Shakespeare and Painter—surely this first dramatization of the *All's Well* story should prove at least as informative an analogue as anything likely to turn up on the banks of the ancient Ganges.

Along with some dimly relevant analogues of other cultures Lawrence also advances works drawn from medieval Europe and therefore of potentially greater significance. But the quest to prove that Helena is as virtuously clever as Griselda is admirably patient begs several questions. First, how do we know that a Renaissance—or even a medieval—audience never shared our own uneasiness over a Virtue Story's carrying its virtue too far or "transgress[ing] the most elementary demands of common-sense and decency in making for its goal"?[21] Boccaccio certainly seems to be encouraging a "modern" common-sense response when he has his narrator begin and end the tale of Patient Griselda with lengthy editorializings over how differently Gualtieri's "mad piece of stupidity" should have been resolved.[22] Nor does Lawrence's picture of a society unruffled by "fantastic exaggerations" tally with Boccaccio's closing picture of the women among the group who "fell to discussing" the story: "For a long time, some took one side and some the other, one blaming this and another praising it."[23] Granted, the audience within the *Decameron* was probably more sophisticated than many frequenters of the Globe. But when Lawrence claims that a "very considerable part" of Shakespeare's audience "looked to the stage to tell them the tales which they knew, and resented, just as children do today, any radical alterations,"[24] we must notice that he fails to document his condescending portrayal. Even more patronizing is his view of Shakespeare knuckling under to these childlike militants, never daring to break with earlier forms of any romantic story lest he risk a bad gate. Only in *Troilus and Cressida* did Shakespeare "undertake the perversion of a romantic tale," and that treatment, Lawrence hastens to explain, "was not of his own choice. . . . The tale had already been perverted" by Henryson and others.

The freedom Lawrence denies Shakespeare and allows Henryson suggests that whereas it requires a great artist to make a common story memorable, it is often the lesser writer who more profoundly influences the development of that story's meaning. If Shakespeare were free only to follow an inferior's lead, then Accolti, as we shall see, might easily replace Henryson as the perverter of this romantic tale. But have not the greatest artists of every age always viewed traditions as challenges to innovate? They and their mediocre fellows are equally "of an age" in the sense they all spoke to issues their era considered relevant and alleged to be timeless. But great writers are also "for all time," and their art has endured precisely because they thought and felt more profoundly than their contemporaries. Whereas commonplace opinion may fully explain the works of commonplace minds, it can never explain more than the artist's point of departure, an assumption, for example, so widely held as to elicit questions from a person dissatisfied with the obvious. To ignore one of the most pervasive Elizabethan critical commonplaces, the writer's obligation to imitate his models *creatively*,[25] is both bad history and the beginning of bad historical criticism. Shakespeare was not free to be incomprehensible to his audience, of course, but when we approach his plays with expectations nourished by their sources, we often find those expectations quickly overturned. When Shakespeare "allows the original moral" of the *Othello* story "to degenerate into an aspect of the partial or evil interpretations put upon the events by disaffected or incompetent observers,"[26] he is making Cinthio's story his own through what contemporary critics called "stepping beyond" or "wading farther," in this case radically altering his model's point of view.

If it is dangerous and sometimes anachronistic to patronize first the audience and then the writer, it is equally misleading to oversimplify the writer's sources. To make complete sense out of the *All's Well* story, we must render intelligible every contribution, from the tale told within a fourteenth-century Italian villa to John Florio's oddly bowdlerized "translation" of 1620. But the very process of defining the tradition, of setting up like things in chronological order, encourages us to emphasize similarities and discount differences, slighting contributors Shakespeare may have carefully studied but apparently did not borrow from. We do Shakespeare a disservice if we ignore what he rejected without reasoning the need; we do his creditors a disservice if we measure them only in terms of what was taken from them and consequently overlook other brave, new things they may have been attempting. We shall never gain a close sense of the story's provenance or "coming-forthness" until we are content to treat each writer with reference to what he had to work with but irrespective of the consequences he helped to shape.

Of all the contributions prior to Shakespeare's, Boccaccio's tale of Giletta has been most often discussed and oversimplified. Whereas few recent critics believe that *All's Well* is fully explained by Lawrence's analogues, no one has rejected his more basic and therefore more dangerous oversimplification of Shakespeare's ultimate source. Hence, while the meaning of Helena's story is increasingly argued, the meaning of Giletta's is still consigned to the nursery. Even so generally astute a critic as Madeleine Doran seems haunted by Lawrence's Clever Wench when she insists that the only problem in *All's Well* "is Helena's problem of getting the man she wants for a husband," a "problem in wit, not in manners or morals. The clue to it is in Boccaccio's heading to the tales of the third day," which tells us that " 'under the rule of Neifile, discourse is had of the fortune of such as have painfully acquired some much-coveted thing, or, having lost, have recovered it.' "27 Here indeed is an important clue, a fact that must influence our inquiry into the meaning of any story related during Neifile's reign. Clues are but servants to answers, however, and before assuming, with Doran, that the heading poses "a fairy-tale problem" requiring "fairy-tale solutions,"28 we must ask several questions. Does so straightforward and general a topic as how the coveted was acquired or the lost recovered necessarily establish a fairy-tale problem? Or is it not rather an invitation for a great variety of tales? In what sense can the conclusions to stories other than the one about Giletta be called fairy-tale solutions? Finally, if the set topic allows—indeed, actually inspires— very different stories, why is the desired or lost "thing" always sexual?

We may end up with a tale of multiple meanings, none simple or romantic, some even contradictory. Each meaning must be noted, however, not only to do Boccaccio justice but to re-create all possible avenues of creative imitation as they might have appeared to those who followed him. And if each writer does not solve all our problems with his predecessor, he will certainly help us ask the right questions of his successor. When we reach *All's Well,* we may not, like Doran, believe that "we are thrown off the track" by Shakespeare's "fault" of developing "far more character in Helena and her mother-in-law than we have need of for the story."[29] If we have allowed the contributors to shape the tradition, we shall be on a different track and probably see a different story.

Our study of the story Shakespeare received and enriched will therefore begin by noticing how differently even its first full-blown treatment can be interpreted (Chapter II). Since Boccaccio is careful to establish a great deal of dramatic and thematic interplay in the *Decameron*'s opening days, it is quite possible that the meaning of Giletta's adventure was supposed to be affected by the tales that surround it. There is certainly strong evidence that the straightforward story Queen Neifile apparently had in mind when she proposed the Third Day's topic has a difficult time making its virtue clear amid her subjects' satiric excursions, a context that Boccaccio is purposefully manipulating.

From the wit and irony of mid-fourteenth-century Italy we shall proceed to a more dignified, aristocratic treatment of late-fifteenth-century France, *Le Livre du Très Chevalereux Comte d'Artois et de sa Femme*[30] (Chapter III). Evidently written partly to compliment the houses of Burgundy and Artois by inventing illustrious deeds for their ancestors of the preceding century, this anonymous chivalric romance is as "charming" and "graceful" as Lawrence maintains.[31] But if Boccaccio's irreverence was overlooked or rejected by the elegant chronicler, we need not assume, with Lawrence, that he is wholly uncritical of his characters' behavior. The bed-trick, insists Lawrence, was never regarded as "immodest, unworthy of a refined woman"; would the courtly historian "have attrributed this ruse to the elegant and virtuous Countess [of Artois] if it had seemed indelicate?"[32] We might just as easily argue that the loyal and pious narrator condones his hero's attempts to seduce the Princess of Castile and his wholesale abandonment of former loyalties for selfish pleasures. Sympathetically yet disapprovingly the chronicler must truthfully report an unheroic lapse in the history of the House of Artois: "Et au voir dire, le conte avoit si mis en obly son pays, sa femme et aultres choses quelconques, qu'il ne luy chailloit que de mener la joyeuse vie ou royaulme de Castille."[33] Given her husband's lust, her own long-suffering love, and the unavailability of *delicate* ruses, the Countess's means of recovering her husband seems both immodest and winsome, especially since the marriage she saves was not, as in all other versions, an enforced union.

If the most fitting word for the French romance is "charming," "cynical" is the aptest description of the next version of the *All's Well* story, Bernardo Accolti's *Virginia,* a comedy to honor the wedding of the Sienese magnifico, Antonio Spannocchi, in 1494 (Chapter IV). Celebrated as "the unique one" by men now better known than he, including Ariosto and Castiglione, and constantly intriguing for favors at the courts of popes and princes, Accolti's own career no doubt influenced his dramatization of Giletta's adventures. One of Accolti's few modern readers speaks of Virginia's "grovelling self-abasement" and "excessive astuteness,"[34] attributes certainly implying that at least one of Boccaccio's successors did not see Giletta as simply and senti-mentally as recent critics. The evidence that Accolti knew of the French romance is weak, but his indebtedness even to Boccaccio's themes and tone is quite clear. When the play concludes by reluctantly honoring a heroine who has triumphed with a pious deceit, "con pietoso inganno,"[35] we are reminded that the Third Day's deceptions are always sexually motivated and usually religiously rationalized. Besides supporting an ironic reading of Boccaccio and contradicting Lawrence's contention that no analogue places the bed-trick in an immodest light, *Virginia* also points forward. Scenes, characters, and themes Shakespeare allegedly invented are also found in Accolti, the most interesting of which is possibly the model for Parolles, Ruffo, who feeds his master's amorous hopes with empty words ("tu pur mi pasci di parole").[36]

Before attempting a new historical-critical reading of *All's Well* (Chapter VII), however, we shall also try to determine what the tale of Giletta meant to writers closer to Shakespeare's time (Chapter V) as well as to examine all nonliterary contexts that illuminate the play (Chapter VI). Sixteenth- and early-seventeenth-century contributors are not as inventive as Accolti and the French chronicler, but the Renaissance view of translation as a kind of creative imitation is fully vindicated by the Englishings of William Painter (London, 1566-67) and John Florio (London, 1620) as well as by the racy French version of Antoine le Maçon (Paris, 1545). Farther from Shakespeare's sphere are the more explicit commentaries accompanying the editions of the *Decameron* in Italian, Girolamo Ruscelli's (Venice, 1552), for instance, whose "pretie notes" Painter himself admits studying.[37]

Equally essential to our discovery of what *All's Well* meant in its own time is an understanding of how (or whether) it reflects contemporary religious and political issues. Helena, for instance, like all the heroines before her, feigns a pilgrimage, but she is the first to mention a specific place. In view of Walter Starkie's observation that pilgrimages to Santiago were ridiculed by both Catholic and Protestant Humanists,[38] Shakespeare's smallest elaboration may speak multitudes. Similarly, several plays contemporaneous to *All's Well* treat the miseries of enforced marriage, an implication that the Court of Wards and Liveries enjoyed even less respect than it had in its first years under Henry VIII. Are these detections of socioeconomic abuses relevant to Bertram's case? Such backgrounds are hardly sources proper, full-blown literary models, but like the obscurest analogue, they could have served as sources of inspiration, springboards for Shakespeare's imagination. At the very least they are for us potential sources of information, hints of what to expect or to look for. In dealing with a play so perplexing, we cannot afford to ignore any gloss upon any part of its long and varied tradition.

NOTES

1. These six categories are outlined and illustrated by Joseph G. Price, *The Unfortunate Comedy,* pp. 133-36.

2. *Shakespeare's Problem Comedies,* pp. 32-77.

3. Robert Ornstein, ed., *Discussions of Shakespeare's Problem Comedies,* p. viii.

4. *The Sovereign Flower,* p. 144.

5. Ibid., pp. 145-46.

6. Cf. Clifford Leech, "The Theme of Ambition in 'All's Well That Ends Well,' " p. 29; G. K. Hunter, ed., *All's Well That Ends Well,* p. xlvii; James L. Calderwood, "The Mingled Yarn of *All's Well,*" pp. 75-76.

7. See Leech, esp. pp. 21-28.

8. Hunter, p. xliii.

9. See Hunter, pp. xlvii-lii, lix; Leech, p. 29. "The old romance is not blended to perfection with the problems of reality," adds, Herbert G. Wright, *Boccaccio in England from Chaucer to Tennyson*, p. 216.

10. II. i. 105 ff. All citations to Shakespeare are to *The Riverside Shakespeare*, ed. G. Blakemore Evans.

11. Knight, p. 150.

12. *MV*, V. i. 3-6.

13. Thomas Speght, ed., *The Workes of our Antient and Learned English Poet, Geffrey Chaucer, newly Printed*, fol. 188^r.

14. Price, p. vii.

15. Ibid., pp. 156-57; the references are to Curtis Brown Watson, *Shakespeare and the Renaissance Concept of Honor*, pp. 183-84, and to Joel Hurstfield, *The Queen's Wards*.

16. Watson, p. 184.

17. Hurstfield, pp. 129, 141.

18. Lawrence, p. 39.

19. Ibid., pp. 237-38.

20. Ibid., p. 41.

21. Ibid., p. 51.

22. *The Decameron of Giovanni Boccaccio*, Trans. Frances Winwar, pp. 649, 659.

23. Winwar, p. 659.

24. Lawrence, pp. 69-70.

25. See Howard C. Cole, *A Quest of Inquiries: Some Contexts of Tudor Literature*, pp. 216-26.

26. Frank Kermode, *The Riverside Shakespeare*, p. 1198.

27. *Endeavors of Art: A Study of Form in Elizabethan Drama*, p. 251. Doran is citing the J. M. Rigg (Everyman ed.) trans.

28. Ibid., pp. 251-52.

29. Ibid., p. 251.

30. Ed. J. Barrois.

31. Lawrence, pp. 45-46.

32. Ibid., p. 51.

33. Barrois, p. 173.

34. Wright, pp. 215-16.

35. *Verginia*, sig. F1^v.

36. Ibid., sig. C3^r.

37. Wright, p. 157.

38. *The Road to Santiago*, pp. 6, 47-55.

II
Dramatic Interplay in the *Decameron:*
Boccaccio, Neifile, and
Giletta di Nerbona

Everyone in the pleasant company was lavish with
praise of the queen's story, especially Dioneo, the
only one still left to speak for that day.
Ladies, he began, after many compliments, something
in the queen's tale made me change my mind, and
I've decided to tell you another story instead of the
one I had intended.

Decameron, II, 10

Because the ninth story of the *Decameron*'s Third Day is
generally regarded as the sole source of *All's Well That Ends Well,* it is
not surprising that more has been written about Giletta by Shakespeareans than by students of Boccaccio. And since Shakespeareans
necessarily tend to examine what Boccaccio did mainly in terms of
what was done to him, not what he was attempting in his own right,
their comparisons usually leave us admiring Shakespeare's complexity
and patronizing Boccaccio's simplicity, his "clear, simple" plot and
characterization, the "archaic charm" of his "artless, undemanding
manner."[1] Whether the tale of Giletta is "a simple story about love
and courage"[2] or "a simple tale of reconciliation effected through
circumstance,"[3] it is always essentially "a folktale by a master of
rapid narrative with the simplicity and emphasis upon action to the
disregard of motivation or psychological probability that is characteristic of the kind."[4] Criticism from W. W. Lawrence to Clifford
Leech affirms the "strong element of folk-tale romance" that Shakespeare assimilated from Boccaccio, and even Herbert G. Wright excuses

Helena's bed-trick as "merely part of the machinery derived from . . . the incredible world of romance."[5] But E. M. W. Tillyard's answer to "how Boccaccio coped with his inherited fairy-tale material" is probably the most explicit: "all he aimed at was a diverting story that would not overtax the powers of a lively and critical audience to suspend willingly their disbelief. So he contented himself with keeping the characters simple, with inserting a few realistic touches . . . and with taking the fabulous lightly."[6] From critics who approach Boccaccio through Shakespeare, then, there is at best an appreciation of a good yarn well spun. When we turn to character or theme or mood, however, simplicity is the key. The meaning of Helena's story is reserved for scholars; the meaning the Giletta's is a matter for children.

In view of the witty, urbane society portrayed in the *Decameron,* it is surprising that the alleged simplicity of III 9 has scarcely been challenged even by those who approach Boccaccio as more than a lively recounter of folktales. Mariella Cavalchini's "Giletta-Helena: Uno Studio Comparativo" examines "queste due versioni *ugualmente geniali* di un medesimo tema"[7] without denying either artist his own sense of design, but since Boccaccio's design is supposedly to celebrate the triumph of Giletta's "volontà," we are back to Lawrence's folktale heroine, the Clever Wench. And though S. Bernard Chandler shows how frequently Boccaccio has the "savio" upended by love and other emotions, the story of Giletta, that "savia donna," is noted to exemplify "the cool use of the brain to grasp the reality of a situation, . . . to devise plans accordingly and to carry them out effectively."[8] We have been recently encouraged to see the story of Alatiel (II 7) as a parody of the Greek romances,[9] to view the exploits of Masetto (III 1) as "a deflation of the courtly love mystique"[10] and to enjoy Frate Alberto's courtship of Lisetta (IV 2) as a facetious tribute to the stilnovist *donna angelicata.*[11] Granting such evidence of parody in the tales surrounding III 9, and with an eye to the dramatic and thematic interplay Boccaccio is so obviously exploiting in the first few days, we shall see that Queen Neifile's account of Giletta is neither simple folktale nor conventional virtue story. Read in the context Boccaccio provides, it becomes an ironic part of a satirical whole that repeatedly unmasks religious rationalizations.

The topic for the Third Day has of course been often noted, but almost invariably as the first step toward oversimplification. We have already seen that tales illustrating how the desired was achieved or the lost recovered need not deal with fairy-tale problems and solutions.[12] Instead, the great variety of stories the set topic theoretically allows and actually inspires suggests that Boccaccio, like his great English contemporary, Chaucer, wanted more than a handy realistic framework into which he could insert thematic groupings of stories culled from reading and conversation. He also wished to achieve a dramatic interplay between his characters and between their offerings as a means of enriching specific stories. The meaning of each tale would thus be conveyed partly by the announced topic, partly by the personality of the narrator and his response to the preceding story, and partly by any unannounced similarities that emerge as the day progresses. For the First Day, of course, no theme is set. "I'll leave each one free this first day to choose whatever subject he pleases,"[13] rules Queen Pampinea. But we must notice that the edict's phrasing was probably intended by the queen to inspire in her subjects (and very likly meant by Boccaccio to suggest to his readers) certain limitations of subject matter in the days ahead. Moreover, despite the freedom allowed them, every teller labors to point out some element in the preceding tale that reminded him of his own. And it soon becomes difficult not to believe that Boccaccio is calling our attention to the awkwardness of these transitions and the speciousness of the accompanying editorializings.

Reflecting upon wicked Ciappelletto's beautification, for example, Panfilo concludes the opening story by suggesting that although this evil man is likely in the devil's hands, "we may appreciate the goodness of God toward us in regarding the purity of our faith and not our error whenever we make an intermediary of His enemy, thinking him a friend" (p. 12). Since the story has actually demonstrated the human habit of being deceived by mere words—the French thought *cepperello*, a fungus, meant chaplet (thus ironically anticipating the fungus's sainthood), and the credulous Burgundian friar never questioned his deathbed confession—Panfilo's moral postscript seems comically inappropriate. Neifile, however, continues this thread of dubious editorializing, first echoing Panfilo's sentiments regarding "the goodness of God" and then turning from a fraudulent saint to a corrupt papal court: realizing that the Church flourishes despite its own shepherds' attempts to undermine it, Abraham embraces Christianity. Though Neifile's example of God's goodness concludes with a brief comment on the Jewish convert's holy life, the emphasis of her story is no more complimentary to the faith ostensibly celebrated than Panfilo's. Boccaccio's amusement over his narrators' tendencies to make virtues of necessities becomes apparent when Filomena launches into her story about another Jew (I 3) by noting that "we have been hearing many fine things about God and our faith" (p. 16), an appeal to a framework composed solely of satiric excursions. And if Filomena's purpose is to show "how good sense is the source of comfort," her narrative argues as well for a religious tolerance not extended to Neifile's Abraham. The mood of mischief is finally underlined when the roguish Dioneo prefaces the fourth and only bawdy story of the day by suggesting how easily a determined narrator can transit and moralize: "We have already heard how Abraham saved his *soul* by the good advice of Jehannot de Chevigny, and how Melchizedek by his wisdom guarded his *riches* from Saladin's schemes. Now . . . I'll tell you a short tale of how a monk saved his *body* from unpleasant punishment through his own adroitness" (p. 19; italics added).

It is at the close of the First Day, however, that Boccaccio's desire for dramatic interplay becomes especially clear. The newly elected Filomena has no sooner established the next day's topic than Dioneo, whom "the queen knew . . . to be a merry, spirited rogue" (p. 39), asks to be excused from illustrating any set theme and then, lest any one suspect he begs this favor because he has so few stories at hand, volunteers to be henceforth the last to speak. (Although the queen gladly grants this request, before the Second Day has ended she is given good reason to regret her decision.) The first eight members of Filomena's court faithfully adhere to the topic she has proposed, each informing us of *"someone who after being tormented by various misfortunes achieves at last a happier result than he had hoped for"* (p. 38). The "misfortunes" are indeed "various"—sensual, sublime, solemn, silly—for Filomena, in choosing her topic, meant to honor a sad fact of human experience, man's subjection to all the vagaries of chance. But to what should we ascribe the inevitable "happier result" ("lieto fine")? The madcap Martellino (II 1) is rescued through the efforts of his loyal companions; doltish Andreuccio (II 5), on the other hand, regains his wealth through sheer luck, though when he falls unharmed through the floor of the courtesan's privy, credit is given to God alone. The stories of Beritola (II 6) and Gualtieri (II 8) both follow a well-worn medieval route: momentary happiness, protracted tribulation, a sudden restoration by "God, who when He wills is the unstinting All-giver" (p. 87).

But in the other half of the first eight tales it is impossible to say precisely where credit for the unexpected joy should go. Lauretta is not sure whether Landolfo (II 4) was saved through "God's will, or a gust of wind" (p. 63); Pampinea asserts that II 3 will deal with "Fortune's ways," but the happy end begins when her heroine reasons, " 'God has ordained the proper time for my desires' " (pp. 53, 57). Most amusing are the couplings of those divinities which shape the events of II 2 and II 7. It is only "by divine providence" that Rinaldo d'Esti regains his stolen property, yet he is careful to thank both "God and St. Julian" (p. 52), perhaps because Filostrato, in innovating upon the set theme, proposed to show the value of Saint Julian's Paternoster for those who venture through the uncertain lands of love, perhaps because Boccaccio, in dealing with the patron saint of hospitality, has stressed the sexual solace of the widow's hospital. The events of the story and the comments it evokes both underline the moral that God worked through His saint, and Julian, through the lady's desires: Filostrato's audience "gave thanks to God and St. Julian for having come to [Rinaldo's] rescue in his sorest need. Nor did they think the woman foolish for taking advantage of the bounty God had let fall in her very house" (p. 52).

There is finally the world of Alatiel, where "St. Julian" is replaced by "blessed Saint Increase" (p. 94). Panfilo's purpose in relating his story at first seems as conventional as the morals of the tales that precede and follow it: since no one is "entirely exempt from the pranks of Fortune," we should "simply resign ourselves to accept and make the best of what God has granted us, for He alone knows our needs, and can bestow them upon us" (p. 89). But the commonplace is facetiously applied as Panfilo first accuses his "charming ladies" of seeking more beauty than has been granted them and then proceeds to the misfortunes of lovely Alatiel as a warning against such sin. By the end of his exemplum, however, Panfilo is willing to settle for a lesser moral—"A mouth crushed with kisses loses no boon"—and Boccaccio tells us that at least some of the ladies may have "sighed as much out of yearning for such frequent nuptials, as out of pity for the princess" (pp. 107-8). Given the roles each divinity plays, the mixed response is understandable. It is "Fortune" who drives Alatiel from one lover to another, who makes the girl her "plaything," and in whom she eventually takes pleasure (pp. 93, 100, 103); it is "God" to whom the sultan commends his daughter at her departure and offers thanks for her safe return. But it is also "by the aid of God" that Antigonus rewrites Alatiel's history, including her devotion to "Saint Increase-in-the-Hollow," and it is to "the grace of God" that she in turn ascribes her rescue by Antigonus (pp. 104, 106). Between the stories of Beritola and Gualtieri, which show how God used Fortune to manage happy conclusions, Boccaccio reveals how one lady, who never aspired to anything, "made the best of what Fortune had set in store for her" (p. 100) and eventually used God to excuse her not wholly unfortunate experiences.

Realizing that she has granted Dioneo the privilege of speaking last, Queen Filomena proceeds to illustrate her own topic with the story of jealous Bernabò and his faithful Ginevra, the germ of Shakespeare's *Cymbeline*. The popularity of this tale in Boccaccio's own time has long been accepted,[14] and even the narrator hints at its conventionality in her preface: "There's a popular saw often quoted to the purpose" (p. 121). "While keeping to the set theme," then, Filomena will also verify a piece of folklore—the deceiver always ends at the feet of the deceived—and thereby warn the "dear ladies" to be on guard. It is easy to see how neatly the tale measures up to the day's theme: Ginevra is the *"someone . . . tormented"*; a credulous husband and his treacherous companion make up the *"various misfortunes"*; the *"happier result"* is achieved through a resourcefulness and self-assurance as obvious as Ginevra's alias, Sicurano da Finale. The proverb is also verified when Ambrogiuolo is finally unmasked and dispatched to a horrible death. But how applicable is this tale to the queen's dear ladies? Since Ambrogiuolo never even confronts, much less tempts, the heroine, and since he deceives her husband with little difficulty, Filomena's warning would have been better directed at the three men in her audience.

This minor disparity between prefatory claim and actual story

immediately pales, however, as Dioneo begins wrenching both to fit
his own designs. "Something in the queen's tale," confesses Dioneo,
has led me "to tell you another story instead of the one I had intended.
I'm referring to Bernabò's simplemindedness . . . and the stupidity of
all men who think the way he did, fancying that while they go about
the world having a good time with this wench and that, their wives
remain at home with their hands in their laps" (p. 132). Given the tale
Filomena has actually told, Dioneo has some right to complain about
Bernabò's stupidity. Yet Dioneo deliberately misunderstands the
central moral when he excludes the extenuating circumstances that
encouraged Bernabò's folly and then redefines that folly by echoing
Ambrogiuolo's cynical argument—what trust can frail men place in
frailer women? No matter that the queen has stressed the deceiver's
cunning, not the husband's simplemindedness; no matter that she has
shown us a hero who is definitely not sporting with this wench or that,
and a heroine very much at home with nothing in her lap but her hands.

But Dioneo's specious application is not the only element conspicuously at odds with the queen's solemn instruction; the story he is
suddenly reminded of mocks the very topic she has proposed. Serious
or merry, with or without a sexual basis, and capitalizing upon the
power of God or Fortune or amusing combinations thereof, all nine
tales do illustrate the set theme along fairly straightforward lines. With
the possible exception of II 7, where happiness consists of sex with
respectability, the vitality of each narrative draws upon an unexpected
event that restores the sufferer to his original contentment, perhaps a
little older and wiser, but enjoying essentially the same things he had
lost. Dioneo voluntarily subjects himself to the topic with the following
results: the *"someone tormented"* is Bartolomea, one of Pisa's most
handsome girls and the unwilling bride of an aged judge; the *"various
misfortunes"* that torment her are single—and obvious; the *"happier
result than . . . hoped for"* is her most fortunate kidnapping by the
virile pirate, Paganino, who frees her from the judge's perpetual
fast days and Lenten vigils. When an escape is finally offered, the lady
embraces what would normally be considered misfortune and sneers
upon both restitution and husband, who is left coining his own proverb,
"A bad hole wants no vacation."[15]

Whether the Second Day's theme has been enriched or simply degraded, it has obviously been given a clever twist. And whether Boccaccio wanted the reader's sympathy to remain with Filomena's view or to shift to Dioneo's or to rest somewhere between, it is important to notice that the sympathies of the immediate audience are completely overturned. "So you see, my dear ladies," concludes Dioneo, with a parting shot at the queen's story, "when Bernabò argued with Ambrogiuolo, he only succeeded in riding the nanny-goat down the precipice." To which Boccaccio then adds: "The story had set them all laughing until their jaws ached, and with one accord the ladies said Dioneo was right, and that Bernabò had been a fool" (p. 138). Has Boccaccio arranged the Second Day's storytelling at its queen's expense or should we discount this mischievous interplay as a passing and somewhat misguided interest in local color?

The drama continues for several pages, in any case, and Boccaccio takes some pains to make sure we notice it. Immediately after Dioneo upends her story and apparently her topic, Filomena appoints her successor, Neifile, whose first official act is to set aside the next two days, Friday and Saturday, for prayer, fasting, and cleansing. Having just heard so much about fasts and vigils as the "fairy tales" through which the impotent "convert others to their own deficiencies" (p. 132), a different queen might not have risked listing the reasons why these days should be kept sacred. But this is anxious, reverent Neifile, the only woman originally opposed to including the young men in the ladies' company for fear of scandal, whose first story shows how God works even through His corrupt Church and whose second allows a "mocker of God and his saints" a happy end only after a severe beating (pp. xxxiv, 12 ff., 44). But if—perhaps because—Neifile is prone to timidity, she greatly admires active, forceful people, a characteristic revealed not only in her choice of heroine for her third story, but in the topic she selects to accommodate it. And therefore her second official act is to rule that while each tale shall once more treat a "phase of Fortune," it must also show how *people . . . through their own efforts . . . obtained something they wanted very badly, or got back what they had lost"* (p. 139). During the Third Day, then, we shall again hear of Fortune's quirks and final joys, but this time the agency through which the happy ends are achieved should not be open to question—"except Dioneo, of course, who is privileged to tell whatever he pleases."

Long before we hear from Dioneo, however, we sense the emergence of similarities more specific than those required of the Third Day's storytelling and very likely less complimentary than those Neifile had in mind when she sought a proper context for her celebration of resolute Giletta. Neifile asked that the *"obtained something"* be *"wanted very badly,"* but not that it be invariably sexual. Neifile wished to honor human *"efforts"* (though Branca, I, 308, n. 6, reads "industria" as "ingegnosità" or "abilità") and her companions respond with protagonists whose ingenuity is always disingenuous. And if the queen was looking ahead to her heroine, whose designs would be blessed by God, many of her subjects look back to Alatiel, who used God as an excuse. It is of course Boccaccio, not the king or queen his characters elect, who actually sets each day's thesis, arranges for unannounced topics to emerge, and works toward ends none of his sovereigns could have possibly foreseen. As a raconteur, Boccaccio had hundreds of stories at his disposal; as an artist, he selected, refurbished, established relationships between, and thereby lent new meanings to those frequently told tales. The Second Day's thematic and dramatic interplay is achieved mainly through the narrators' varied and sometimes mutually exclusive explanations of how the happy end was achieved, and it culminates in Dioneo's suggestion that one person's misfortune may be another's greatest happiness. In the Third Day an even richer interplay is attained as the narrators' illustrations of "industria" become increasingly relevant to that exhibited by Giletta, and Dioneo again crowns the whole with the bawdiest story in the *Decameron.*

That Boccaccio wanted religion to play a major role in the Third Day's tales is evident at the outset. Filostrato, "in keeping with the given theme," opens with the story of Masetto, a vigorous young laborer who feigns dumbness in order to gain employment at, and hence entrance into, a convent, where he allows himself to be successively seduced by eight nuns and eventually by their abbess. His duties finally proving too demanding, he abandons his disguise, and it is soon rumored among the local folk that the gardener had been cured "by virtue of the nuns' prayers and the grace of the convent's patron-saint" (p. 149). When we realize that Boccaccio's main source, the "novella di messer Roberto" in the anonymous *Novellino,* sets the gardener among a countess and her ladies,[16] who found a convent only after losing their honor, we might ask why the locale was shifted to a nunnery. One reason is immediately clear. The religious setting allows Boccaccio to enrich the tale with *double entendre;* in one special sense Masetto actually was cured "by virtue of the nuns' prayers." Nor could the gardener of the *Novellino* boast that "that was the way Christ treated those who adorned His cap with horns" (p. 149)

But it is only as we continue through the Third Day that we are likely to notice another reason for its tales' customarily religious contexts, the emergence of a theme that supplements the announced topic of gaining or regaining. In at least four of the eight stories preceding Neifile's, we find sexual desire donning a religious mask; the other four, including III 1, sooner or later set the events in a religious (or sacrilegious) perspective. As a result, a structural miracle, the tale's cleverly contrived resolution, is usually accompanied by a thematic miracle, the illusion of divine intervention. Whether we discover a lustful lady, *"by means of a sanctimonious confession"* (p. 154), turning an obtuse friar into her unwitting bawd (III 3) or watch a clever abbot translating a farmer to purgatory in order to enjoy his wife (III 8), we eventually catch a familiar refrain: There's a divinity that shapes our lecherous ends.

Since the headnotes to the tales preceding III 9 reveal the sexual goal each protagonist seeks and the specific pretense he employs, a few remarks concerning additional evidence of dramatic or thematic interplay should suffice. Pampinea's story of Agilulf's groom (III 2) is intended to show "the cunning [of] a fellow of even less significance than Masetto" (p. 150), whom Filostrato had used to prove that the coarsehanded are rarely dullwitted. Since the groom displays considerable ingenuity not only in impersonating the king in order to lie with the queen but also in escaping detection, Pampinea has evidently attempted to satisfy both options implicit in the set topic, though what is acquired (sex) is not what is recovered (safety). She is the only subject to make the attempt, however, and it is hardly surprising that only the one who set the topic is able to illustrate both gaining and regaining with a single *"something . . . wanted very badly."* Pampinea is also the first narrator to use a bed-trick, though Neifile's handling of this well-worn device is closer to Fiammetta's (II 6). Finally, despite the fact that neither of the groom's stratagems evokes a religious mood, Pampinea asserts that the king's good sense was displayed in his benediction: " 'Let him who did it, not dare to do it again. Now go, and God be with you' " (p. 153). What God has not prevented, the king cannot wholly amend. Yet the blessing is also a warning, and if the groom does not repent, he at least reforms. Most important, according to Pampinea, is that Agilulf stopped the affair without harming his wife's reputation. Boccaccio has been less gentlemanly, for the historical Queen Teudelinga (Theudelinda of Bavaria) was regarded as a lady of "rare and most laudable piety."[17]

Because the first two tales have revealed the ingenuity of humble folk, Filomena presents the third "not merely to continue the established sequence" (p. 154) but to prove that the supposedly learned can be tricked by creatures even as simple as women. The secondary thesis necessitates a female protagonist (the only one to appear until III 9 and III 10) and a male as sexual object. Since the lecherous lady uses the confessional to complain about misdeeds she hopes to inspire, no tale takes God's name in vain more frequently, and the witty mock-piety is enforced by Filomena's conclusion to the adultery achieved through the sacrament of penance: "may God in His great mercy lead me quickly to it, and all other good Christians who are so inclined!" (p. 162). Filomena's prayer and her heroine's wit are of course both highly commended by Dioneo, and Panfilo continues with a tale quite similar in mood, theme, and tone. Despite his attractive wife, Puccio's only desire is to attain sainthood. After his friend, a clever young monk, reveals the secret exercises through which the Pope himself manages a short cut to blessedness, Puccio engages in some spiritual heroics while the monk enjoys his wife. Her final words, "You've made Puccio work out a penance, but it has certainly given us our heaven," simply echo Panfilo's claim concerning people "who by their own efforts to attain to heaven, unconsciously pave the way for others" (pp. 162, 166).

Elissa's tale of Il Zima (III 5) also emphasizes the paradise of love fulfilled, but in a solemn, almost idealistic manner. Boccaccio seems to imply that something new is at hand when Elissa begins to speak "rather saucily" of those who were fooled by themselves in trying to fool others. Few noblemen in the *Decameron* are less noble than the husband of Il Zima's beloved. If Il Zima's goal is sexual, it is no passing passion; if he intends to gain by his gift, his giving is prompted by covetous Francesco; and if he must wear a mask to effect his dialogue-of-one, it is because Fancesco has broken the spirit of their agreement. Nor may we dismiss the religious language (and hence the religious perspective) of Il Zima's plaints as the conventional overtures of courtly-love hyperbole. His courtliness and love are both genuine. The lady is indeed his "treasure, [his] soul's only hope," and because of the sincerity of his longings she begins to "feel what she had never before experienced—love itself!" (p. 169).

Having paused only long enough to prove that even a sexually motivated pretense can be portrayed sympathetically, Boccaccio returns to his exposures of clever conniving with protagonists and plots more and more similar to Neifile's. In her story of Ricciardo and Catella (III 6), Fiammetta, like Elissa, intends to show how a reserved lady, "terribly afraid of love, was made to taste its fruits by the cleverness of her lover" (p. 172). But the differences are far greater than the similarities. Here there is no covetous, jealous husband. Filippello, apparently loved by Catella, is introduced primarily to explain her insane jealousy, and it is this vice that insures the success of Ricciardo's bed-trick. Il Zima taught his lady the meaning of love, and she granted her favors voluntarily; Ricciardo teaches Catella the dangers of darkness and disguise, and the meaning of love is sensual and ironic. After suffering her supposed husband's embraces, Catella gives vent to the rebuke she has been savoring, keynoted by "But praise be to God and my foresight" (p. 177). Realizing the truth, her indignation is greater: "I don't know how God will give me the fortitude to bear the insult and the trick you subjected me to" (p. 179). If God does not help, Ricciardo does, and Fiammetta concludes with a prayer that her audience's joys in lovemaking may equal her characters'.

Fiammetta's closing prayer is of course repeated verbatim[18] at the conclusion of Emilia's story of Tedaldo and Ermellina (III 7). Although the only tale that focuses on regaining, its end is the same and its method is an especially cunning employment of religious hypocrisy. Still hoping to recover his mistress, Tedaldo comes back to Florence "disguised as a pilgrim on his return from the Holy Sepulchre" and convinces her that he is "a prophet" sent "from Constantinople . . . at God's prompting" (pp. 181-82). "Look[ing] his holiest," the lover confesses his beloved in order to ascertain the sin for which God is certainly punishing her, and when Ermellina reveals that she was frightened from adultery by "a scurvy friar," Tedaldo, still disguised, cries out against the hypocrisy of such religious orders. And it is Tedaldo's sermon that makes Emilia's tale almost twice as long as the others told on the Third Day, a barrage of mischievous illogic that Dioneo must have envied. With helpful Tedaldo's glosses, Ermellina learns that it was not her affair God was punishing, but her infidelity to her lover, and the parody of pulpiteering concludes as the pilgrim hurries off to the husband he will resume cuckolding: "I am a friend of yours, Aldobrandino, sent for your salvation by the Lord, who was moved to compassion by your innocence" (p. 189).

If Ricciardo's sexual stratagems point back to the groom's bed-trick, Lauretta's story of Ferondo's purgatory (III 8) reminds us of Puccio's penance and Felice's paradise. The narrator, on the other hand, claims that she has been inspired by Emilia's account of Tedaldo's supposed death. But there are more relationships between the seventh and eighth narratives than Lauretta mentions. Prior to the story of Giletta, no tale exploits so fully the motif of shaping divinity, and it is Tedaldo, not Don Felice, from whom the abbot inherits his pious mask and rhetorical prowess. "Don't reject the bounty God is sending your way," cautions the abbot, and with a logic as specious as the pilgrim's he convinces Ferondo's wife "of the rightness of the deed" (p. 197). After their first interview, "marvelous were the things she told of the abbot's holiness"; after many months she conceives, and his miraculous ability to recall her husband from purgatory "added inestimably to the abbot's reputation for holiness" (pp. 197, 202).

By the time the queen's turn has come, then, the meaning of the tale she offers to satisfy her own topic is bound to be colored by her subjects' satiric excursions. If we allow Boccaccio a sense of design beyond that which he allows his narrators to comment upon, the increasing emphasis upon God as a sealer of sexual bargains leads us to question whether there is more to Giletta's story than Neifile realizes. In observing how Neifile's subjects define the topic's "industria," we have yet to encounter a fairy-tale problem or solution. And instead of what the set theme might have evoked, a series of virtue stories related only through the announced topic, we have found usually bawdy and sometimes ironic treatments of the unannounced theme of disingenuous ingenuity. As a result of this thematic interplay, we think less about the teller and his tale as an independent unit and more about Boccaccio refurbishing stories, creating characters to tell them, and finally arranging these parts into a thematic whole. He implies as much when he has Neifile preface her tale by calling attention to the order of her subjects' contributions. Unwilling "to infringe upon Dioneo's privilege," the queen wishes that someone else were left to succeed Lauretta: "How can any story we can tell sound like anything after Lauretta's? It's a good thing she was not the first, or few of the others would have cut any sort of figure, as I'm afraid will be the case with those still left for to-day. Well, anyhow, I'll tell the first story that comes to my mind" (p. 203).

Is this merely an instance of fourteenth-century *sprezzatura*? Or has Neifile sensed that after determining the theme (and probably her illustration of it) some unsympathetic treatments have intruded? In either case, Neifile seems bent upon insuring our approval of Giletta's virtue as well as her wit and perseverance. The queen is the first narrator not to grant at the outset that the protagonist's goal is sexual, glossing over Giletta's desire as a "more fervent and boundless love than is common with children"; it is only when the king's disease gives her heroine a "suitable pretext" (cf. "onesta via," Branca, I, 419) to travel to Paris that she admits Giletta's "love . . . grew more and more ardent" (p. 204). True to the spirit of her topic's "industria," Neifile is also careful to set her story within a rational, realistic world. Her heroine's love may be remarkable, but no mystery is attached to the king's illness or to the medicine Giletta prepares: "Profiting by the knowledge she had gained from her father, she prepared a powder ot various herbs, beneficial to what she believed to be the king's malady" (p. 204).

The problem is that Neifile will not let well enough alone. In attempting to make Giletta more virtuous than the protagonists of simple virtue stories, she feels obliged to invest both gaining and regaining with religious sanctions. It is during the story's two critical moments, when Giletta tries to have or hold her unwilling husband, that we hear the most about God and are most likely to recollect the sanctimonious

102634

LIBRARY
College of St. Francis
JOLIET, ILL.

fakery of the preceding stories. When Giletta's "powder of various herbs" is first mentioned, for example, we may not be reminded of that "powder of extraordinary virtue" (p. 198) by which the abbot dispatches and recalls his mistress's husband from purgatory. But Boccaccio soon underlines the similarities when he has Neifile add to Giletta's equipment two powers equally marvelous. No longer hopeful of being cured, the king refuses to see his doctors. When Giletta asks to examine him, however, he makes an exception on the not very logical ground that she is "young and attractive" (p. 204). But since the most famous physicians have failed, even her physical attractiveness does not gain her his leave to undertake a cure until she claims divine credentials: "Need I remind you tht I don't heal by my art alone, but with the help of God and the learning of . . . my father. . . ?" (pp. 204-5). The king is not impressed by her father, though a "famous physician." For him it is rather a leap of faith: "Then the king pondered: 'Perhaps this girl has been sent me by God.'" By anticipating the king's restoration with such religious glosses, Neifile attempts to seal her heroine's first design with God's approval. Even disdainful Beltramo is obliged to bring God into play, arguing that such a mixed marriage is againt his will ("già a Dio non piaccia che io sì fatta femina prenda giammai"; Branca, I, 422).

Through Giletta's deeds and Neifile's glosses, however, Beltramo must accept this "mere she-doctor" as the pleasure of God as well as of the king. Still chafing over the enforced marriage, Betramo rides off to the Tuscan wars, while Giletta, hoping to recover him "by acting tactfully," restores order to Rossiglione and gains his subjects' love. Neifile also encourages our sympathy for her heroine when she has Giletta offer to leave Rossiglione rather than remain to bar its lord, and Beltramo responds "harshly" with his "two almost impossible demands" (pp. 206-7). The obvious pathos of Giletta's leave-taking—her recounting "piteously what she had already done for love of the count," her decision "to spend the rest of her life in pilgrimages and works of charity, for the good of her soul" and her request that her husband be informed of her resolution never to return—draws many tears from her new subjects. But while Neifile strives for poignancy, she must also prepare for Giletta's next move with facts less heartwarming. The tearful farewell is part of a larger plan, the pilgrimage is for the health of something other than her soul, and immediately after having commended her subjects "to God's keeping," she hastens to Florence and Beltramo. Having gained her husband through a "powder" similar to the guileful abbot's in the eighth tale, she will regain him with a pilgrim's mask like lusty Tedaldo's in the seventh and by means of a bed-trick reminiscent of lecherous Ricciardo's in the sixth.

Once in Florence, God's hand is increasingly visible. "By some strange chance" Beltramo happens by the inn where Giletta, only the preceding day, happened to lodge, and her hostess chances to know of his love for her neighbor's daughter. Still disguised as a pilgrim, Giletta visits the woman, reveals her own situation, offers a large dowry, and finally proposes the bed-trick. The woman, initially fearful of such a large undertaking, soon agrees that both end and means are honorable ("onesta cose . . . ad onesto fine"; Branca, I, 428). Like the king, Giletta's earlier agent, the woman puts her faith in the heroine's God— "Who knows, but God may grant me the grace of conception?"—and Neifile once more proves that this faith was not misplaced: "By God's will, the countess became pregnant of two sons, as her delivery revealed at the proper time, during those first embraces which the count so passionately craved" (pp. 209-10). But again Neifile goes too far. Beltramo has demanded a son fathered by himself; Giletta must have nothing less than twins. And notice how she proves that conception occurred on the very first night. Has she forgotten that such careful arithmetic can be misleading? Lauretta has just finished her story by explaining why Ferondo never became jealous: the abbot's son was born "at the proper time, according to the opinion of fools who think a woman must be exactly nine months gone with child before she delivers" (p. 202). For Neifile, however, nothing remains except to show how Beltramo accepted God's will. Giletta soon realizes she is pregnant and rewards the woman; "Thanks to the Lord and you, I have obtained what I was after" (p. 210). After bearing Beltramo's sons, she returns to Rossiglione in secret and awaits an opportune moment. Beltramo obliges Neifile's theme by selecting All Saints' Day for a great feast, and it is against this emotional backdrop that Giletta makes her entrance, "in her pilgrim's garb as usual" and begging "in God's name" that her husband honor his agreement.

In a world in which the wonders of God are directly performed and

where even the nobility join the humble heroine's tearful pleading, it
is difficult to reject Neifile's conclusion that "thenceforth, he honored
her as his wife and loved and cherished her above all else" (p. 211).
All stories told on the Third Day conclude happily-ever-after, but
usually because the protagonist is rewarded for his cleverness, not his
goodness. From a strictly moral perspective, in fact, many of the decent
characters end up less happily; it is at their expense that the desired
was acquired or the lost recovered. By having her protagonist continually speak of and ostensibly gain God's aid, Neifile is the only narrator
to attempt a reconciliation of wit and virtue, to celebrate ingenuity
and resolution within a moral frame of reference. And had Boccaccio
not decided at the close of the First Day to let Dioneo always have the
last word, we might infer that Neifile's touching illustration was intended
to represent the topic's final and loveliest meaning. But Dioneo once
again uses his prerogative to malicious advantage. So relevant are the
misadventures of Alibech (III 10) to the story of Giletta that we can be
fairly certain of several things. First, Neifile should have been far more
concerned about the tale that followed than about the one that preceded her own. Second, the awkward similarities between the events of
III 9 and those of III 6-8 are not the figments of an overripe critical
imagination. Third, whatever Boccaccio's view of the set theme's final
meaning, he leaves his characters puzzled, debating, dramatically
involved.

In exploiting the new turn taken by Neifile's sanctification of "industria," Boccaccio has Dioneo first remind us of the "effetto," the theme
or spirit, of the day's tales:

> Dioneo had listened attentively to the queen's story, and seeing
> that it was over and he alone remained, he proceeded with a
> roguish smile, without waiting to be asked:
> Perhaps you've never heard, most gracious ladies, how the devil
> is put back into hell, so I'm going to tell you, without getting too
> far from the spirit of to-day's story-telling. Besides, the informa-
> tion may help you save your souls. . . . [pp. 211-12]

Since the antecedents of Alibech's story amount to no more than a few
sketchy analogues,[19] it is only Dioneo's "roguish smile" ("sorridendo")
and his wrenching of the preceding day's topic that would lead his

audience or Boccaccio's first readers to expect something other than serious instruction. Although Dioneo goes on to claim that he will also show love's power over the humble, this does not necessarily negate the remark about "sav[ing] your souls"; Neifile has just finished mingling matters spiritual and amorous.

It is rather in the hyperbolized idealism of the tale's opening that we first sense the mischief. The beautiful young Alibech often listens to the Christians of Barbary praising "the Christian faith . . . and the delight of serving God," and when she asks "how He might best be served wih the least trouble," she is directed to follow those who have forsaken the world for the desert solitudes of Tebaida (p. 212). "It was no reasoned urge that led her on, but a mere childish whim," explains Dioneo, with perhaps a glance at Giletta's "more fervent and boundless love than is common with children." Nevertheless, this "very ingenuous" (cf. "semplicissima") girl manages a most arduous journey and, having arrived, explains to each holy man in turn that "she was inspired by God, . . . yearning to be of service to Him, and in search of someone to show her how best to serve Him" (p. 212). Of all the recluses, only Rustico, "a devout youth, and the soul of sanctity," volunteers to undergo the temptation of sharing his cell with her. His resolution is of course vanquished before the first night has passed, but in order to enjoy the innocent girl "without rousing in her mind any suspicion of his lecherous purpose," he makes her "believe she was doing it all in the service of God" (p. 213). And once "the most pleasing service she could render the Lord" is defined as "put[ting] back the devil in the hell to which He had condemned him," we are hardly surprised to find a plethora of religious metaphors flavoring the account of Alibech's initiation into Rustico's Tebaidan mysteries, those rituals leading to her eventual enlightenment: "I really think all people are fools, who spend their time at anything but the service of God" (p. 214). All that remains for her to learn, concludes Dioneo, is that such worship is ecumenical.

To what extent does Alibech's quest enrich the Third Day's topic? "Attentively" has Dioneo listened to a tale of how a young lady (the first female protagonist since III 3) gained her desire with and through God's blessing; "with a roguish smile," he presents another young lady who acquired what she wanted allegedly with and through God's blessing. The unannounced theme of hypocrisy that emerges in the first eight tales is amply illustrated in "dissoluto" Rustico. But Alibech is no hypocrite. Being "semplicissima," she cannot recognize, much less confess, her "childish whim," and we leave her to glorify God as sincerely in Neerbale's bed as she ever did in Rustico's. In her honest confusion of sexual and divine service, Alibech seems to point back to Giletta, a heroine equally sincere though not quite so obviously misguided. Certainly it is no coincidence that the Third Day ends with a pair of heroines who gain and regain sexual ends while their narrators stress their innocence. As he re-establishes the day's earthy mood, then, Dioneo also reflects Neifile's etherealizing. In order to annotate Giletta's self-deception, "onesta," Neifile's favorite word, becomes "semplicissima." More important, Alibech, unlike the protagonists of the first eight tales, first obtains a *"something* [she never dreamed she] *wanted very badly"* and then, having lost it, *"got* [it] *back* [whence she never expected]*."* Does she do this *"through* [her] *own efforts"*? Alibech makes it difficult to discuss "industria" without "sorridendo."

Viewed against Neifile's topic and illustration, the result of Dioneo's decision not to get "too far from the spirit of to-day's story-telling" should tell us how far Boccaccio has himself departed from fairy- and folktales. The dramatic interplay of the Third Day's closing moments is as sophisticated and complex in mood and tone as the thematic relationships conveyed from tale to tale. Dioneo concludes by asking the "dear young ladies, who are badly in need of God's grace," to gain His favor as Alibech did, "since it's highly agreeable to the Lord, and a joy to both parties—besides, much good might come of it" (p. 216). If the women's need for God's grace is meant to remind us of Dioneo's moral preface—"the information may help you save your souls"—his reference to the "much good" that might come or be born ("molto bene ne può nascere"; Branca, I, 439) of sexual-divine service could be a last glance at the means through which Giletta secured her happiness. Neifile, wondering whether one wolf will shepherd the sheep better than the sheep have directed the wolves, presently crowns the first king, Filostrato, who replies that he would have the wolves teach the sheep what Rustico taught Alibech. That will only be, retorts Neifile, twisting Filostrato's own story, when you have learned what the nuns taught Masetto, and recover your tongue at the cost of your bones.

But if the characters continue to tease one another, Boccaccio concludes by teasing us. Always unfortunate in his own romantic affairs, Filostrato rules that the Fourth Day's tales shall celebrate lovers who met unhappy ends. The plaintive mood is enhanced as Lauretta, at the king's request, sings of her own unrequited love. The song is sorrowful, yet lovely, even haunting in its tenderness. The spell is quickly broken, however, as Lauretta's audience hastens to interpret what can only become less beautiful for the glossing: "All of them had paid special heed to it, but interpreted it differently, some going so far as to think it meant, according to the Milanese, that a good hog is to be preferred to a jolly lass. Others, however, gave it a more ethereal, better and truer significance, which it is not necessary to mention here" (p. 219). Granting the amusing interplay between the characters and between their treatments of the set theme, the rather cavalier conclusion makes good sense. Each of the Third Day's stories is capable of being interpreted in the Milanese manner, yet few, if examined independently, could not also yield meanings more sublime.

The real question, however, is whether Boccaccio encourages us to interpret any part without regard to the whole. The "more ethereal, better and truer significance" of even a relatively independent song "is not necessary to mention" or recite ("recitare non accade"; Branca, I, 445). What is actually to Boccaccio's purpose is conveyed by "recitare," especially in its more modern, theatrical sense, and revealed in his decision to spell out an earthy proverb and leave us guessing about a truer significance, perhaps confused but certainly involved. The bawdy, idealistic, ethereal, and ironic responses to the announced topic's "industria" also imply that Boccaccio's interest does not really lie in the "truer significance" that may be derived from a single story. His energies are rather directed toward a significance more dramatic and probably even truer, the meaning that cannot be derived from an individual tale until the rest have been read.

Boccaccio's personal view of Neifile and her story is of course impossible to document. But we can agree that the stories surrounding Neifile's savor more of fat hogs and jolly lasses than the sublimer glosses the omniscient author never feels obliged to make explicit. The more we attend to the interaction of tales and tellers, the more complex each story appears, especially the supposedly simple yarn about Giletta di Nerbona. Thus the first contributor to the *All's Well* story seems at first to suggest and then to deny a single, sympathetic point of view. An idealistic treatment requires a heroine who is unquestionably virtuous in both the modern and archaic senses, righteous as well as powerful or effective. For this kind of heroine we must proceed to northernmost France, and well into the following century.

NOTES

1. Geoffrey Bullough, *Narrative and Dramatic Sources of Shakespeare,* II, 378-79.

2. John Arthos, "The Comedy of Generation," p. 102.

3. Harold S. Wilson, "Dramatic Emphasis in *All's Well That Ends Well,*" p. 222.

4. Ibid., pp. 222-23.

5. See Lawrence, *Shakespeare's Problem Comedies,* pp. 39-63; Leech, "The Theme of Ambition in 'All's Well That Ends Well,' " pp. 19 and passim; Wright, *Boccaccio in England from Chaucer to Tennyson,* p. 215.

6. E. M. W. Tillyard, *Shakespeare's Problem Plays,* p. 95.

7. P. 320, italics added.

8. "Man, Emotion and Intellect in the *Decameron,*" p. 400.

9. Stavros Deligiorgis, "Boccaccio and the Greek Romances," pp. 97-113.

10. Howard Limoli, "Boccaccio's Masetto (*Decameron* III, 1) and Andreas Capellanus," p. 287.

11. Louise George Clubb, "Boccaccio and the Boundaries of Love," pp. 188-95.

12. See p. 7 above.

13. *The Decameron of Giovanni Boccaccio,* trans. Frances Winwar, p. xxxviii. Although I use Winwar's Modern Library Edition throughout this chapter, all citations have been checked against Vittore Branca's two-volume ed. of the *Decameron.*

14. Cf. John Colin Dunlop, *History of Prose Fiction,* II, 73-75; A. C. Lee, *The Decameron: Its Sources and Analogues,* pp. 42-57; Branca, I, 275, n. 1.

15. "Il mal furo non vuol festa," but Branca, I, 305, n. 1, also suggests "foro" for "furo."

16. See *Le Cento Novelle Antiche,* ed. Letterio di Francia, pp. 101-3.

17. See Dunlop, II, 81.

18. As Branca, I, 378, n. 6, points out, both tales end with "Iddio faccia noi goder del nostro."

19. See Branca, I, 432, n. 1: "Gli antecedenti indicati per questa novella sono scarsi e assai vaghi, per non dire inesistenti."

III

Customs Holy and Wholly Gallant:
Le Chevalereux Comte d'Artois

> Et ce qui frappe le plus dans *le chevalereux conte
> d'Artois,* c'est surtout cette abnégation de soi, et ce
> dévouement à la chose publique qui ne connoît point
> de bornes, ainsi que ces révélations fréquentes sur
> l'alliance hybride de pratiques religieuses et
> d'habitudes toutes galantes.
>
> J. Barrois, Introduction to *Le Chevalereux Comte
> d'Artois*

No story in the *Decameron,* not even the last day's most winsome portrayals of magnanimity, quite prepare us for the gentility and guilelessness of *Le Livre du Très Chevalereux Comte d'Artois et de sa Femme.*[1] The Countess of Artois, whom Barrois salutes as "cette héroïne de la foi conjugale" (Introduction, p. viii), enjoys an aura of sympathy Neifile never manages to create for Giletta, partly because the marriage she saves was never, like Giletta's, enforced, and partly because her chronicler harmonizes or obscures the discords Boccaccio emphasizes. The Countess's world is larger and more sophisticated than Giletta's, but it is also more sincere; among its hordes of embattled infidels there is no spirit so profane as Dioneo. The point of view is no longer alternating and contradictory but single, steady, and straight-forward. Gone is the quizzical tone and atmosphere of dramatic immediacy; when the objective, authority-laden historian becomes nostalgic over those distant events he had promised only to report, we look in vain for Boccaccio's thin smile. Most conspicuously absent is the *Decameron*'s mood of mischief, evidence that supports the conjectures of several nineteenth-century scholars that both Boccaccio and the anonymous chronicler drew directly and independently from a lost, mid-fourteenth-century French poem.[2]

Like its source, the circumstances under which the romance was written remain obscure. At the outset the historian recalls his happening upon "ung livret" (the lost poem?) that mentions the Count of Artois's lofty enterprises. His own fuller account, evidently inspired by the little book, has been conscientiously if unimaginatively researched, for any faults (and presumably any virtues) in the ensuing pages are entirely owing to the authorities he has slavishly followed: "en ceste petite euvre je ne dois estre réputé que l'escripvaint qui escript ce qu'il trouve ès aultres volumes" (p. 1). This objective stance—Barrois calls it "une candeur toute gothique" (p. x)—is maintained throughout the romance. At least a dozen times the chronicler refers to "l'ystorien" or "l'istoire" to support an opinion or to excuse a missing detail; even more frequently, however, he achieves a narrative economy by putting aside his role of scribe and admitting or implying that he has had to abridge his sources.[3] And sometimes it is difficult to determine whether the chronicler or his authority has taken sides: "et tient l'istorien que ce [paralyzing grief of the Saracens upon discovering their dead] fut la principale cause qui saulva *nos crestiens* de grant inconvénient" (p. 111; italics added).

We shall better understand the chronicler's purpose if we bypass his confessions and examine his distortions of history. The very title of his work is a polite fiction. Philip I, born in 1323 to Eudes IV of the illustrious House of Burgundy and Jeanne de France, Countess of Artois, would have inherited his mother's title had he survived her.[4] But he died one year before her at the siege of Aiguillon (1346), much too young to have managed one-third of the feats attributed to him. At fifteen he married Countess Jeanne, "Fille au Comte de Boulogne," as the subtitle claims, and four years later she bore him a son, his only heir, as the chronicler's authority witnesses: "et ne trouve mie l'ystorien qu'ils eussent plus d'ung enfant" (p. 195). This respect for the truth, however, quickly passes in the closing picture of Philip of Burgundy and his wife aging gracefully in peace and love, blessed by God and their subjects, and mourned for in their passing by their son, who was fortunately "tout fourny et parvenu en seignorie"

(p. 195). Why has the chronicler ignored Philip's death in his son's fourth year, Jeanne's remarrying to become Queen of France, and Philip II's dying in his late teens, having survived his mother by only one year? Since happy endings are not dictated by the conventions of chivalric romance, the fictional conclusion should probably be viewed as the final compliment to a later Duke and Duchess of Burgundy, who had already enjoyed Philip's outrageously unhistorical rescue of Castile from the Saracens.

Such a conjecture is supported by several of Barrois's observations (pp. xvii-xviii). Among the many bizarre ornaments in the manuscript's margins he notes one enclosing this tribute: "Rodulf, marquis de Axberg, conte de Neuchastel, de Rothelin et de Luzemborg." We know that Rodulf of Axberg (or Rodolphe de Hochberg, 1427?-87) was a close friend of Burgundy's last duke, Charles le Téméraire, or the Rash (1433-77), in whose name he governed Luxemburg. We discover Rodulf's arms not only among the marginal devices on almost every leaf but even upon the hero's shield and banners in many of the manuscript's richly embellished miniatures. Rodulf's wife, Marguerite, daughter of William of Vienne, is similarly flattered when the chronicler turns from Artois's accomplishments to salute "le prince de Vienne, qui jeusne et biaulx chevalier extoit sur toute riens, tant noble" (p. 76). Yet another kind of compliment is found in the conjunction of Rodulf's monogram with that of Marie of Savoy, who married his son, Philip, in 1476. It was, in fact, for this marriage, according to Barrois, that the older of the two extant manuscripts was probably executed.[5]

To understand the chronicler's purpose most fully, however, we must notice how frequently he pays court to his patron's patron, the adventurous prince who led the pride of Burgundy, including Rodulf's son, to the disastrous Battle of Nancy (1477). Surely the glories allegedly achieved by Philip of Burgundy in the 1340s were at least partly inspired by the glories Charles the Rash aspired to in the 1470s. The chronicler's wearisome attention to banquets and tournaments, for example, seems less strange when we find his contemporary, Olivier de la Marche, devoting two-thirds of his account of the Duke's whole reign to the ceremonies at Bruges in 1468, when Charles married Margaret of York.[6] Similarly, there seems to be a connection between Philip's and Charles's crusades. During the Feast of the Pheasant at Lille (1454), Charles had sworn to God, the Virgin, and the pheasant that he would expel the Turks from Constantinople. But the battles he fought over the next twenty-two years were for his own phantom kingdom of Lotharingia, a state that would embrace all the Burgundies of the past, an empire that seemed assured until the debacle at Morat in June, 1476.[7] To the warrior whose motto remained "Je lay emprins," Philip's fictitious expulsion of the Saracens from the Peninsula could have been a reminder tht Constantinople was still occupied.

It is of course impossible to determine how much of the chronicler's manipulation of the past was designed primarily to point up the present. The disguised Countess of Artois is introduced to her wayward husband as "ung jeusne compaignon de Picardie, nommé Philippot," and she soon becomes his "varlet de chambre" (pp. 136-37). Was the Countess's alias intended merely to suggest the conviviality she exudes or also to compliment the famous Burgundian seneschal, Philippe Pot?[8] More important, even the most conventional aspects of the Count of Artois's chivalry may have reminded Charles's subjects not so much of courtly literature as of a real court that continually strove to enact that literature.

Given the political situation in northern Europe in 1476, however, we may be reasonably certain as to how a Burgundian responded to several significant passages. Like the chronicler's perfect knight, Charles "adoulçoit les furieux, humilioit les orgueillieux, [et] appaisoit les désacordez" (p. 3). Unfortunately, many of the proud whom Charles had to humble were his own not-very-loving subjects of Holland, Flanders, Brabant, Liege, and Lorraine. Since royal entries into their cities were sometimes effected only by first leveling the walls, Charles's court must have looked wistfully upon the picture of Philip's welcome to Cardonne: "Les cloches sonnoient, clers, presbtres et aultres vindrent audevant d'eulx chantans hympnes et louenges à Dieu, et le commun peuple crioit haultement: Vive le noble conte d'Artois! vive fleur de proesse, mirouer de noblesse! vive le plus vaillant de cest monde! Benoist soit de Dieu celluy qui de noz ennemis anciens nous a deslivrez!" (p. 121). Similarly, whereas Charles was never fully at peace with his cousin, Louis XI of France, Philip finds in Paris "le Roy, qui luy fist grant chière, et ainsi firent tous les princes, seigneurs et chevaliers de la court pour le beaulx renom qu'il avoit. . . . Et . . . comme patron de chevaliers . . . par l'espace d'ung moys . . . il séjourna en la cité" (p. 33).

Perhaps a final historical gloss will help to explain one of the chronicler's most curious fictions. Students of the *All's Well* story are likely to approach *Le Chevalereux Comte d'Artois* by way of either Boccaccio or Shakespeare. In either case, they expect to find a French king disparaging one of his wards, the future Count of Roussillon, by forcing him to marry a commoner from Narbonne. Instead, they discover in Artois a mature hero who dearly loves and wins a lady of his own rank and leaves her only after their marriage proves childless, a mighty warrior who has the kings of France and Castile as admirers, not guardians, and a tireless champion whose quests eventually bring him to "Nerbonne, . . . la derrenie ville du royaulme," where he hears how "le prince de Castellonne faisoit forte guerre au conte d'Urgel et de Roussillon, seigneur de Parpignam" (p. 34). This initiates a twenty-eight-page episode—more than one-eighth of the romance—in which Roussillon is rescued through Artois's skillful and courageous soldiership. Since the episode is entirely fictitious, and since the fiction could have been set in any of those countries Philip traverses on his journey southward, one wonders whether Roussillon came in by way of the chronicler's "aultres volumes." Or did he start with Boccaccio's tale, changing people and places to flatter Charles, and eventually, out of an odd respect for the source he had abused, bring in the old hero as someone at least meriting the new hero's rescue?

Probably the best reason for setting Philip's first great victory in Roussillon, however, is hinted at when the chronicler finally explains that his hero acted "pour l'amour de l'ancienneté du conte d'Urgel et du bon droit qu'il y avoit" (p. 59). Here again the history of the 1340s seems to have been rewritten to reflect several extremely complicated relationships of the 1460s and '70s.[9] Both Charles and Louis had designs upon Roussillon, then part of the Principality of Catalonia in the Kingdom of Aragon. As early as 1461, the year Louis ascended the throne, a marriage was proposed between Charles's daughter, Mary of Burgundy, and Ferdinand, son of John II of Aragon. Temporarily straining Aragon-Burgundian relations was another alliance concluded between John and Louis the following year, through which Louis gained Roussillon and Cerdagne from Aragon in return for pledging to put down the Catalan revolution. Fearing Louis as much as John, the Catalonians turned to the Constable of Portugal, Dom Pedro, heir to the ancient title of Count of Urgel and nephew to Charles' mother, Isabella of Portugal; until his death in 1466, Dom Pedro's campaign in Catalonia was supported by Burgundian troops. When the Catalonians next turned to Louis's uncle, René of Anjou, Charles forged new and stronger alliances with John (1469, 1471). By 1473 John had recovered Barcelona and Roussillon, and Charles was promising his not-so-faithful comrade-in-arms that he would help raise the French siege of Perpignan. The siege was in fact lifted later that year, but through some unromantic negotiating between Charles and Louis that gave Roussillon neutral status. In little more than another year Roussillon was again occupied by the French, thanks to Charles's ill-conceived betrayal of John and Spain's preoccupation with the Castile succession.

Affairs like this lead one modern historian to conclude that "there was very little to choose as far as duplicity was concerned between the Valois of Burgundy and the Valois of France."[10] The less objective chronicler, on the other hand, ignores recent Burgundian pragmatism in order to re-create its glorious past: "Le conte d' Artois oyant cest nouvelle [that Perpignan was being besieged], conculd [conclut?] de servir et aidier celuy à cuy le droit seroit" (p. 34). What the chronicler ignores, of course, he cannot be ignorant of, though it may be difficult for us to believe that even in the face of his own day's widespread opportunism he could be so confident that princes of the preceding century acted solely according to "le droit." Despite the contemporary problems he occasionally touches on, however, the world he memorializes is basically of the past, once very real but now irrevocably lost. It is therefore not only an earlier Duke of Burgundy he is idealizing but his times and customs. At the outset he returns his audience to chivalry's golden age with a mixture of pride and regret: "Ou temps passé que noblesse et honneur séoient ou plus hault degré par toutes régions crestiennes, et que parfaicte proesse estoit entée et enracinée au plus fort ès cuers des nobles hommes, pour les faire luire et seignorier au monde par l'excercite de chevalerie, qui les faisoit eslever jusques à la félicité de glorieux renom, estoit ung conte en Artois . . ." (p. 2).

Against this kind of setting we can better understand the chronicler's reworkings of contemporary events. His main purpose in making Philip's age so exemplary is not to ridicule Charles's, even less to flatter it. His confidence in the "parfaicte proesse" of Artois's time seems as sincere as many a modern American's belief in the virtues of his own country's founding fathers. And therefore, if certain battles Philip allegedly fought strongly resemble those Charles actually faced, it is probably because the chronicler, again like his American counterparts, tends to imagine how present problems would have been solved in earlier, simpler, and more virtuous times. Never does Philip relieve the distressed without first assuring them that "Dieu vous aidera de sa grace, selon vostre bon droit; et moy avec les miens vous aiderons . . . en faveur de noblesse et de chevalerie" (p. 36; cf. pp. 50, 59, 66, 86, 112).

It is to the chronicler's credit that he develops his world's moral-religious mood without the ponderous moralizing so common to his era. Editorializings about "ainsi va de ce monde communement" (p. 77) are few, brief, and to the point. His narrative is much more often sprinkled with folksy maxims like "il convient de tel boys comme l'on a, faire le feu" (p. 95) and even his hero is not above "disant avec le prouverbe" (p. 110). He has both the soldier's appreciation of military strategy, always explaining in great detail how Artois arranged his charges, ambushes, and retreats, and the epic poet's eye for grandeur, allowing Artois's Saracen enemies, for example, to deify his skill: "Fuyons! fuyons! car veez là le Dieu des crestiens qui se combat pour ceulx de sa loy. . . . Et à vous dire, son corps y fut tant redoubtez que . . . le disoient estre faé ou homme immortel, car jamais n'avoient veu le pareil" (pp. 95, 97). Above all, both the historian and his hero are generous in their opinions of others. Artois is unwilling to kill one foresworn knight "pour la vaillance qu'il trouvoit en son corps" (p. 72) and his chronicler shows how the Saracen Lord of Gibraltar, "comme vaillant chevalier qu'il estoit" (p. 114), inspired his people.

For all his humane judgments and concerns, however, the chronicler knows exactly where Truth resides and fully expects God or the Blessed Virgin to order its ultimate victory. Between the romance's introductory episodes on how Artois came to love and then leave his wife (pp. 2-32) and its concluding section on how she regained him (pp. 125-96), we are given three extended illustrations of how the hero's chivalry maintained God's right: Urgel is rescued and Perpignan relieved from Castellon's persecution (pp. 34-61); the Countess of Cardonne is proved innocent of the Lord of Moncade's slander (pp. 62-84); Castile is delivered from the Saracens (pp. 85-124). And if in each illustration the moralizing is short, the moral is nevertheless quite clear. "Et de mon costé," Artois promises Urgel, "feray tant adonc, à l'aide de Dieu où j'ay ma créance, que vous aurez bon compte de vos ennemis et plaine victoire" (p. 50). The same focus on considerations holy and wholly gallant is found in Artois's explanation of his arrival in Castile: "je . . . fus informez de la guerre que vous fait le roy de Guernade, payen et ennemy de nostre loy, pourquoy je, desireux de servir Dieu mon créateur, et garder la foy qu'il nous a bailliée contre les mescréans, jusques à la mort, vous suis venue aidier de mon corps en ceste guerre" (p. 86). And though Artois does not reveal to the Countess of Cardonne's squire how God will defend "le droit" in her case, he urges him to trust in Providence: "Laissiez vostre dueil, mon amy, et vous actendés à Dieu, qui garde et deffend le droit d'ung chascuin, car il luy aidera et pourverra bien de sa grace ainsi comme besoing sera" (p. 66).

The moral-religious frame of reference that is thus continually yet unobtrusively developed in the romance's lengthy middle (pp. 34-124) is of course bound to affect our interpretation of its beginning and end, the framework that comprises another version of the *All's Well* story. We must grant at the outset that the first half of this framework is largely conventional, sometimes almost tedious: the doughtiest of knights wins the fairest of ladies while excelling at her father's tournament. The chronicler enjoys Artois's dramatic entrances as stranger knight (pp. 12-16, 24-25) as well as the ironic exclamations of the women in the audience that "bien estoit tel champion digne de belle dame avoir" (p. 14), but neither tournaments nor banquets are nearly as interesting as the first part's final episode (pp. 28-32), in which the husband's desertion of his wife is treated with a sympathy unique to the *All's Well* tradition.

Although Artois's grief over being childless is introduced with an economy verging on abruptness—after the wedding festivities the Count

"retourna en sa ville d'Arras, où il trouva sa bonne et belle femme,
avec laquelle il fut joyeusement par l'espasse de deux à trois ans sans ce
qu'il en eust nulz enfans, dont il en vivoit en plus grant afnoy et des-
plaisance" (pp. 27-28)—the chronicler's description of his leave-taking
is far less hurried. The Countess, quickly sensing the grief her husband
would conceal, begs him to reveal its source, "Monseigneur et chier
amys, je . . . vous supplie très humblement que me dictes la cause de
vostre ymaginacion, car se Dieu plaist et il m'est chose possible, je y
mectray tout mon pouvoir à vous en mectre hors" (p. 29). And though
Artois at first makes excuses, desiring "appaisier sa femme par belles
et fainctes parolcs," hcr "angin subtilz et langue atractive," coupled
with his realization of her "loyaulté et bonne volenté," lead him to
confess that he plans never to return to her until "trois choses qui
sont comme impossibles soient advenues" (p. 30), her obtaining from
him, without his knowledge, his charger, his most prized diamond,
and a child.

   At this point the chronicler's moral framework temporarily works
against his hero. However reluctant and "compassionate" his cruelty,
Artois barely maintains his integrity before his lady's loving indictment:
"Hélas! monseigneur que sur toutes choses j'ay amé et mis paine de
complaire et obéir. . . .[S]embleroıt par ce que ma mort voulsissiés
avancier, ou que ce fust ma coulpe. Si vous prie, en l'onneur d'icelluy
Dieu qui sans pechié nasquit, et sur tout l'amour que vous avez eust
à moy vostre espousèe, et par les courtoises compaignies que nous
avons ensemble se doulcement nourries, que vous ostés de vostre cuer
ceste desraisonnable despartie" (p. 31). Given the cruel fact of Artois's
desertion—a fact upon which the rest of the romance depends—the
most the chronicler can do for his hero is to offer mitigatory evidence.
If the Countess's "regretz estoient tant piteux que chascuin plouroit,"
the Count, feeling the same "grant pitié" but also "tout plain de grant
coraige et homme constant," insists that he departs neither for "mal ne
désobéissance" in his wife but to honor his own vow. And if he
leaves "au grant desplaisir de son peuple," within several lines the
chronicler has brought him to Paris, where everything "qu'il faisoit
plaisoit à Dieu et au monde" (p. 33).

   For the next ninety pages—nearly one-half of the romance—the
chronicler studiously avoids even hinting at the Countess's existence.

But he has not forgotten her. Beginning with the heroine's offer to help
the hero "se Dieu plaist et il m'est chose possible" and extending
through the hero's repeated assurances to the oppressed that "Dieu
vous aidera . . . selon vostre bon droit" (pp. 29, 36), the chronicler
prepares us for those wonderfully ironic scenes in which the oppressed
heroine asserts her own "bon droit" and, helped by the very God the
hero urges others to trust in, easily accomplishes the "choses qui sont
comme impossibles." The chronicler's desire to exploit these ironies
is apparent even in the haste with which he returns to what we thought
he had forgotten. The pagan host is confident of victory, "mais Dieu
de sa grace pourvey aultrement" (p. 118). And no sooner are the
Saracens routed than the Count, with the barest foreshadowing (pp. 85,
90), resumes an interest in "ses nouvelles amours, la belle fille du
Roy" of Castile (p. 122), after which the chronicler turns just as
quickly to the abandoned wife, briefly describing her passage from
grief to hope (pp. 125-28), then her ingenuity and resolution (p. 128),
and finally the long journey to Valladolid that she makes with a faithful
old knight, "le gentilz Olivier," where "firent leur compte d'eulx tenir
d'icy à tant que Dieu pourvoiroit à leur fait" (p. 133).

From this point on the Countess's efforts to reclaim her erring lord
are colored with dozens of references to Providence, many of them
highly ironic. Disguised as "ung jeusne compaignon de Picardie, nommé
Philippot" and content to bide her time wandering through the city
"comme font gens de coustume . . . jouer de lieux en aultre et esbatre,"
the good and clever lady is eventually introduced to her husband and
soon becomes his most trusted servant, "si . . . a Dieu tant aidié"
(pp. 137, 134, 157). Complementing this new direction God's will has
taken are a playful mood and tone hitherto alien to the romance. "Or
me dictes, Philippot," the Count inquires, "estes-vous gentilz-homme?"
"Nanil par ma foy," she replies, "ne suis-je mie." "Et à la vérité," the
chronicler editorializes, "elle ne disoit que bien; mais pour ce qu'elle
le dist tant plainement, il ne y mist point son entendement; ains se prist
à rire, et luy dist: Pensés du bien faire, doulx amis: que Dieu vous
doing bonne adventure et bon jour. Amen, dist la dame, monseigneur,
et qu'à joye vous puisse encoire veoir ou pays dont vous estes seigneur.
Ce ne puet estre, biaulx sire Philippot, dist le conte" (p. 138).

Such ironic exchanges, some whimsical, some bittersweet, keep the narrator's more solemn moments from becoming maudlin. As his "varlet de chambre," Philippot shares her husband's bedroom and therefore cannot help overhearing and responding to his amorous plaints. Here the chronicler becomes as serious as his characters, who now take turns crying out for relief, the Count begging the "vray dieu d'Amours" for pity or death and the Countess, on the other side of the room, appealing more wisely but just as passionately to a truer deity: "Dieu, donne-moy patience que je ne fine ma vie par désespoir! Plaise-toy adoulcir ceste angoisseuse peine . . . car je ne scay à qui recorir, sinon à toy, qui es mon seul refuge" (pp. 145, 147). Within a few pages, however, she has gained her husband's confidence, and solemnity once again yields to wit: "Si ne scay homme céans," confesses Artois, "à qui je voulsisse dire ce que je vous diray, . . . et s'il est ainsi que par vostre moyen je soye allégié de ma douloureuse maladie, je vous prometz . . . que de chose ne me sarés requérir que pour vous je ne face" (p. 151).

Just as the Countess has tracked down her lord through the kindly offices of Sir Oliver, a man known "pour sa bonne grace et preudommie" (p. 128), she now catches him with the help of an equally sympathetic character, the Princess of Castile's duenna, who would not compromise her honor "pour tout l'or de Venise" (p. 158). The willingness of such upright people to deceive the hero for his own good supports the heroin's claim that "Dieu . . . cognoist me bonne et léalle pensée" (p. 159) as well as the chronicler's quest for futher ironic strains. Noticing how courteously the duenna is treating Philippot, for example, Artois sees the long desired tryst materializing and is moved to bless his page for the "bon confort qui à vostre pourchas, si Dieu plaist, m'en venra" (p. 161). Even as the Count hurries to his assignation, he ironically includes friend Philippot in his hope "que Dieu *nous* doing bonne adventure" and, as he leaves her at the door, "la commanda en la garde Dieu" (p. 167; italics added). And it is a grateful hero who admits to his "léal amy Phillipot" the following morning that he could not describe "le disme" of his recent joys, "car je suis parvenu au seul bien . . . et tout par vostre moyen" (p. 170). But the chronicler's most ironic articulation of the theme of shaping divinity comes two chapters later. Having now fulfilled all three of her husband's conditions and planning to hasten home that she might

immediately recall him, Philippot is granted a short leave of absence
and departs with this blessing: "je prie Dieu qu'il vous doing bonne
encontre, . . . que brief nous puissions reveoir" (p. 178).

At its best such irony approaches the fine edge of Boccaccio's, but
nowhere is it employed to question the heroine's ethical or religious
credentials. When "la léale dame sceut véritablement qu'elle estoit
grosse d'enfant," she immediately "loua et regracia le nom du Créateur
qui ainsi l'avoit visitée" (p. 171). If we look for suggestions that such
sincerity is naive or misguided, we find a host of witnesses who imply
the contrary. "De ceste nouvelle oyr fut moult joyeulx le bon Olivier,
et par grant dévocion en remercia et loua le nom de Dieu et de sa
digne Mère" (p. 177). Having been informed of "l'adventure telle que
Dieu et Fortune luy avoient envoyé," representatives of Artois's three
estates journey to Valladolid, hoping through "léal et subtil conseil"
to "ramener [the Count] à raison" (p. 183). It is the leader of this
delegation, the Bishop of Arras, one of the most "facondieux" and
"discret" men of his time, who informs Artois that his wife, "pourveu
de sa [God's] grace . . . est parvenue à l'accomplissement de son
estrange traictié, par son sens, subtilité et perfecte loyaulté" (pp. 184,
187). Somewhat abashed—"se print à muer couleur"—the Count next
hears the duenna praise both "la plus léale et meilleure dame de quoy
l'en puist tenir parole" and, because her plot "n'est en riens mesvenu,
. . . Dieu et la benoite vierge Marie" (pp. 188-89).

Given such incontrovertible testimony, one can hardly blame Artois
for eventually seeing God's hand in the events his wife has so skillfully
managed. It is a genuinely repentant husband who takes leave of the
King of Castile: "et bien considéré, si tiens-je que l'omme qui est marié
ne puet [peut] bonnement ne licitement laissier sa femme sans grant
essoine, qui nulle regle ne observe . . . lui tenir compaignie et payer le
droit de mariage" (p. 190). And it is a genuinely forgiving wife who
welcomes him home: "Dieux! comme fust la contesse esjoye de veoir
son très amé seigneur revenu; baisiers n'y furent pas en chierté, mais en
si grant habandon que l'eaue en la fontaine" (p. 193). If we hope to
find Boccaccio's hints that all may not be well, some irony to qualify
the chronicler's closing picture of the couple living out their lives "en
joye amoureuse ensemble . . . bien contens de la grace de Dieu"
(p. 195), we must make much of one concluding remark: "Toutesvoies,

pour oster toutes suspicions, ainse que Dieu le voult, elle en délivra droit au bout de neuf moys que son seigneur avoit géu avec elle premièrement, dont je ne vous saroye recorder les joyes et les loenges qu'il en fist à son Créateur" (p. 195).

Had we come to this kind of pious observation directly from Boccaccio, we might be tempted to see an ironic interplay between "Dieu . . . elle . . . il . . . Créateur." But an ironic reading of the conclusion makes nonsense of all the fine irony that has preceded it. Here at last the man who has known and shown God's power begins to understand and reflect His grace. It is curious that of all the romance's actions and sentiments, no detail closely paralleling Neifile's story is found until the last paragraph. It is even more curious that the very arithmetic Boccaccio associates with fools is used by the chronicler to reveal God's will. We cannot determine whether such Italian mischief was unknown to the idealistic Burgundian or rejected because it was alien to his design. But we can be more confident concerning Boccaccio's influence on the next contributor to the *All's Well* story, Bernardo Accolti, whose neither holy nor gallant muse celebrated courtesans, popes, and artichokes with equal facility.

NOTES

1. Ed. J. Barrois, whose text is cited throughout.
2. See Gaston Paris, p. 636; Marcus Landau, *Die Quellen des Dekameron,* p. 145; A. C. Lee, *The Decameron: Its Sources and Analogues,* pp. 104-5.
3. Abridgement is admitted or implied on pp. 41, 69, 76, 79, 83, 91, 96, 98, 104, 107, 109, 122, 131, 140, 167, 184, 195; for examples of various appeals to "l'ystorien" and his work, see pp. 22, 36, 57, 80, 84, 104, 111, 180, 195, 196.
4. For biographical details I am indebted to Barrois, pp. 8-11.
5. Barrois collated his text with another belonging to the Bibliothèque du Roy; the latter suppresses one erotic passage, is far less ornamented, and employs a more modern spelling and vocabulary. See pp. x-xv.
6. Joseph Calmette, *The Golden Age of Burgundy,* p. 177.
7. Ibid., pp. 184, 223. See aslo Ruth Putnam, *Charles the Bold,* pp. 415-21.
8. See Calmette, p. 215.
9. Ibid. pp. 237-41, 269.
10. Ibid., p. 269.

IV
Bernardo Accolti's *Virginia:*
The Uniqueness of *Unico Aretino*

Nè altrimenti che nei dì festivi si serravano le
botteghe, correndo ognuno in Castello tosto che si
sapeva che il celeste Bernardo Accolti doveva recitare
al conspetto d'infiniti gran Maestri, e Prelati, con
solenne luminario di torchi, ed accompagnato dalla
molta guardia degli Svizzeri. . . . [N]è prima apparve
nelle reverende Sale di Pietro che il buon Vicario di
Cristo [Leo X] gridò: aprite quante porte vi sono,
e vengano le turbe drento . . . [e] lo ammirando ed
Unico . . . fece in modo restare le genti attonite con
il dove dice . . . che sentissi esclamare dalla pubblica
voce d'ognuno: viva in eterno un sì divino spirito,
e sè solo.

Lettere di Pietro Aretino[1]

No one could have enjoyed the papacy God gave Leo more
than Bernardo Accolti, who stood about among the swarms of poets
lured to Rome by the prodigal liberality of the man "who boasted that
he had been born in a library."[2] While Machiavelli and Castiglione
wrote their classics in enforced retirement, the spirit so divine and so
unique extemporized ephemeras before throngs of admirers and gained
honors denied to Petrarch.[3] Part of Pietro's praise of his countryman—
both came from Arezzo, hence "Aretino"—may reflect their age's
common currency of acclaim, epithets that eventually inflated Ariosto's
"il falgello / de' principi, il divin Pietro Aretino"[4] into *divinissimo,
precellentissimo, onnipotente* and inspired one imperial general to
declare "that the Divine Aretino was 'absolutely necessary to human

life.' "[5] But the era's commonplace hyperbole does not quite explain the singular plaudits given Bernardo, who leads Ariosto's list of over five dozen luminaries, the only man not to share a stanza with others (XLVI, 10-19). Is it not odd that a poet so often ignored in modern histories of Italian literature should appear first among Ariosto's examples of "sublimi e soprumani ingegni," even odder that contemporary celebrations of Arezzo's famous sons[6] should omit the "gran lume aretin, l' Unico Accolti"? We may well wonder how a writer so generally forgotten in our time could have been so widely heralded as unique in his own.

It is another irony of history that Accolti's closest brush with true uniqueness, his comedy of *Virginia,* was evidently unmarked by his contemporaries. They praised him instead as the god of *improvvisatori,* a "nuovo Orfeo" attracting Apollo's envy for creating "All' improviso un stil tanto divino."[7] And the same ready wit, facile learning, and ingratiating mannerisms that went into Accolti's public performances must have also characterized his displays in politer circles, where other Orpheuses were on the make and working just as hard at their own varieties of *sprezzatura.* The documents make it clear that whereas Accolti was occasionally an extemporaneous versifier, he was always a courtier, more typical than unique in his bowing and pushing, flattering and intriguing, a realistic gloss upon the perfect creature Castiglione was in the process of fashioning. In this respect Accolti's life was much like his nondramatic poetry, generally colorful, sometimes spectacular, but almost invariably conventional.

A third and final irony concerning Accolti's significance is less a matter of history than of historical criticism, of our own failure to use the playwright to gloss the greater artists who came before and after him. It is in fact easier to understand the neglect of the *Virginia* in its own time than in ours. Firsthand witnesses can be excused by the excitement of the moment, in which flashy imitations are often mistaken for true originality. From our vantage point, however, we know that Accolti's nondramatic poetry merely advanced that tradition D'Ancona vilified as *"secentismo,"* helping to link the affected metaphors and strained conceits of Tebaldeo and Serafino with those of Marino and Góngora,[8] whereas the *Virginia,* as the first dramatization of the *All's Well* story and one of Italy's earliest high comedies, brings together and comments upon the narrative and dramatic artistries of Boccaccio and Shakespeare.

But neither the *Virginia's* intrinsic worth nor its value in defining its illustrious tradition has inspired serious consideration. As we have already noticed, W. W. Lawrence spends five pages outlining Oriental fairy tales and Scandinavian sagas in order to draw "instructive conclusions . . . as to the general significance" of Boccaccio's and Shakespeare's versions, but he dismisses the *Virginia* in a footnote merely because Shakespeare's dependence upon Accolti has not been proved.[9] Curiously enough, the only provocative comment on this neglected play, one that emphasizes its unconventionality, appears not in a study of Accolti but in a comparison of his source to *All's Well.* To support his contention that both Boccaccio's Giletta and Shakespeare's Helena were meant to elicit our admiration, Herbert G. Wright glances disapprovingly at the "excessive astuteness" and "grovelling self-abasement of Accolti's Virginia."[10] A play centered in the exploits of this kind of heroine certainly suggests that something new, if not unique, is afoot, whether it be a straightforward extension of the medieval virtue story's traditional boundaries or something in a satiric, ironic, or cynical vein, the theme of designing humility. Such a heroine, moreover, implies that a writer close to Boccaccio did not see Giletta as simply and sentimentally as recent critics, though she does lend some encouragement to moderns who have trouble with Helena. Since our view of the whole of the *All's Well* story, not just Accolti's contribution, will be affected by our view of Virginia's character, we must be cautious in speaking of satire, irony, or cynicism. An enthusiasm for discovering the original must be disciplined by a knowledge of what was common, and speculations about Accolti's interests and attitudes should be guided by the facts of his biography. Before examining the *Virginia,* therefore, a brief survey of the traditional aspects of Accolti's life and work seems in order.

Accolti must have thrown in his lot with the courts of central and northern Italy soon after coming of age. Born in Arezzo in 1458 and raised in Florence (where his father, the jurist and historian Benedetto, apparently saw better opportunities), by 1480 he was already in Rome, whence he began what Emilio Santini terms "una specie di vagabondaggio poetico e un po' anche ciarlatanesco" that eventually led to his being "accarezzato e applaudito" at the courts of Urbino, Mantua, and

Naples and by the whole city of Rome.[11] Accolti attracted unsought attention in 1489 for "atti molesti compiuti ai danni di un fiorentino," but by 1494 he had gained the office of Papal Scriptor and Abbreviator.[12] Drawing up briefs for his unsanctified Holiness, Roderigo Borgia, did not prevent Bernardo from currying favor elsewhere. Since the *Virginia* is a piece of occasional drama, a comedy to honor the wedding of the Sienese magnifico, Antonio Spannocchi, in January, 1494, it is unlikely that the playwright would have missed the performance. He also found time to get into trouble again with the Florentine authorities. He was banished for some unexplained wrongdoings that same year, and the peace he later made with the Signoria was forfeited in 1497, when he became involved in Piero de' Medici's attempt to regain the Republic.[13] Among the conspirators beheaded that summer was Lorenzo Tornabuoni, the "thesor de la natura,"[14] according to the sonnet in which Accolti mourns his pathetic death. Bernardo himself was again merely banished and returned to Rome, where the Pope, having just excommunicated Savonarola, was also in mourning. His eldest son Juan, Duke of Gandia, had been assassinated, and among the leading suspects was Juan's younger brother, Cardinal Cesare.

The equally glittering and equally dangerous courts to which Accolti was invited over the next two decades—Milan, Urbino, Mantua, and Naples—are reflected in his sonnets and *strambotti* or folk-lyrics. For he not only celebrated the virtues of the Borgias with courtly poems to chaste Lucrezia, resolute Cesare, and their devoted father; he also sang for a future Pope, Cardinal Farnese, for a recently widowed Neapolitan princess, Isabella of Aragon, for her ambitious adversary, Ludovico Sforza,[15] and for her brother, Ferdinand II, King of Naples, who is given sole credit for expelling the "furor Barbarico" of the French invasion of Italy in 1494 ("Epitaphio del Re di Napoli," sig. F5r). But it was usually love, not war or politics, that Accolti treated, even in his sonnets to a statue and an artichoke. Like his cruel lady, for example, the artichoke she has sent conceals its essence within a thousand deceptions, thrives amid ruins, allows one fleeting favor among so many disappointments (sig. F7r). Similarly, both the Duchess of Urbino and her statue smile but do not answer, quicken the blood only to defraud the desire (sig. F4v).

Given the different kinds of women Accolti worshipped, it is not surprising that the mood and tone of his poetry vary a great deal. Recognizable contemporaries are of course treated respectfully: the two sonnets to Lucrezia contain not a hint of the affair Accolti was alleged to have had with her; several others to the Countess Costanza Vittoria d'Avalos are similarly appreciative yet respectful.[16] And Accolti's muse is most chaste in honoring the grandest of ladies, the Mother of God. In his 172-line "Ternale in laude della gloriosa Virgine Maria" (sigs. G4^v-G7^v), the poet is unquestionably reverential, even though the sense of wonder he would enhance is not helped by his overingenious wordplay and straining of conceits: Mary, like a prism ("saldo vetro"), remained unbroken in the sun's passage through her, begetting the One by Whom she conceived and bearing the One through Whom she was made. But in treating unidentifiable ladies of the present or well known women of the past, Accolti is rarely gallant. To a mysterious Lidia of Florence and an even crueler Giulia there are dozens of despairing plaints. Constant only in her irresistible and unlovely beauty, Giulia is usually deceitful, haughty, and merciless, often sadistic and vicious, and alternately likened to insatiable Death, to the pestilent Dog Star, to a viper in a golden vase, and to the deadliest curse pronounced on any male (sigs. F5^v-F6^v, G1^v-G4^r). Equally grim are Accolti's portraits of the ancient world's famous women: hapless Lucretia, Niobe, and Cleopatra; the not so innocent Clytemnestra, shrinking before Orestes; Helen, who calls herself the ruin of Europe and Asia; shameless Semiramis, justifying incest on the ground that love is never subject to law; an even more reckless Medea, whose murderous passion neither beauty, station, wealth, nor magical potions were able to subdue (sigs. F7^v-F8^v).

Medea's desperate plight—"ma non vinsi amore"—voices a theme Accolti exploits in all but his few political and religious pieces, the power of love to drive, delude, frustrate, and often destroy. The most complex articulation of this theme is of course in the *Virginia*, where the hero's outcries against the destructive heroine are repeatedly followed by the heroine's protests against destructive love. The extent to which Accolti actually experienced those passions he never tired of celebrating is impossible to determine, though the scanty biographical evidence available has not prevented critics from inferrring relationships between the poet's life and his art. Mazzuchelli long ago noted, for example, that Accolti had two children by one of his domestics: Alfonso, who succeeded him as Duke of Nepi, and Virginia, whom he married off to Count Giambatista Malatesta with an exceptionally large dowry.[17] But if the amount of the dowry argues Accolti's love for his natural child rather than his own social ambitions, that affection does not in turn prove that the *Virginia* was named after or in honor of her, as Mazzuchelli and those who follow him suggest.[18] Surely Accolti's allegedly beloved daughter throws as little light upon the play's designing heroine as does his son, Alfonso, upon his dramatic "namesake," the dying King of Naples.

A more difficult question concerning the relationship between Accolti's life and art arises in his sonnet "Della Duchessa di Urbino sculpita" (sig. F4^v), one of the few poems that imply a passionate involvement with a well-known woman of the present. Accolti's "pazzo amore" for Elisabetta Gonzaga merely amused her sister-in-law, that most intellectual of ladies, Isabella d'Este.[19] Nor does Bembo seem to have taken the affair very seriously when he wrote to Bibbiena about the Duchess being frequently courted by "Signor Unico," who, warmer in his old love than the ever-burning lads of seventeen, hopes finally to achieve his goal by moving that heart of stone or at least making her cry.[20] A similar sense of humor seems to pervade Castiglione's account of "signor Unico" and his beautiful betrayer near the beginning of *The Courtier.* Despite such evidence, the most recent study of Accolti detects a note of sincerity in his urbane bantering and witty protestations, assumes that all the anger and bitterness expressed against Giulia were actually directed at Elisabetta, and suggests that his later dream of having his brother, the Cardinal of Ancona, succeed Pope Julius II was fostered only by his desire to make himself worthy of that lady he spent so much of his life pursuing.[21] Earlier criticism, on the other hand, has seldom accused Accolti of any kind of sincerity other than the earnestness with which he played his elaborate game.[22] Art still reflects life, but only in the sense that the partly sentimental, partly aggressive posing within the poems reflects the actual poses through which Accolti achieved his identity at court. Unrequited love kept him dying for thirty years; the ladies continued to listen with delighted astonishment and their husbands, even the impotent Guidobaldo, with complete equanimity.

It is doubtful that the basically serious, idealistic Castiglione found much to admire in such Petrarchan posturings, but *The Courtier* allows every person his say and no document illustrates so clearly that Accolti was actually a player among players, a light turned up and down at the pleasure of his sophisticated circle. "Unico Aretino" initially appears in Castiglioni's cataloguing of courtiers who "spent most of their time" at Urbino during its decade of happiness under the protection of Julius II (1503-13), a period when "poets, musicians, and all sorts of buffoons, and the most excellent of every kind of talent that could be found in Italy, were always gathered there."[23] It is not long, however, before "signor Unico" is given leave to characterize himself, first as a poet, then as a buffoon, and finally as a curious composite of each. Although some suspect that his sonnet on the "letter *s* . . . that the Duchess is wearing on her forehead" is too "ingenious and polished" to have been improvised, this initial attempt to dazzle his circle is "praised with merry applause" (pp. 22-23). But during the next two evenings he is less successful. His witty interruption—Federico's "great burden" is merely to belabor the obvious—is promptly squelched: "You indulge too much in extremes" (p. 96). Even less heeded is his mischievous misappropriation of Plato's *Republic* (V, 3) to counter the view that the Court Lady should not engage in certain bodily exercises: "With the ancients it was the custom for women to wrestle naked with men, but we have lost that good practice, along with many others" (p. 210).

It is during the waning moments of the third evening, however, when he matches wits with Emilia Pia, that the grand poser is permanently silenced. Yet never has the mask of unrequited lover been so courteously removed: "being so very lovable," Emilia insists, you, Signor Unico, are actually loved by many; your "constant lamenting" over ladies' cruelty is, therefore, only a "concealment designed to hide the favors" you have actually received; each woman who has secretly given herself to you is content not only to hear of your unrequited passion but also to watch you "openly show feigned love" to the others. Now if those who you presently "pretend to love are not so ready to believe you as you could wish, this happens because your art of love is beginning to be understood, and not because I cause you to be hated" (p. 268).

While Urbino thus controlled Arezzo's shining light, Leo X's Rome let it blaze unchecked. And yet if Accolti's presence was no more impressive than Castiglione allows and his unrecorded inspirations no better than his extant lyrics, it is difficult to understand the sensation he created. Mazzuchelli and Tiraboschi both attempt charitable evaluations, yet both sooner or later agree with the essentially unsympathetic criticism of Accolti's near contemporary, Benedetto Varchi: after the passing of Dante, Petrarch, and Boccaccio, the Florentine style of writing began to change, and so much went from bad to worse that it became almost unrecognizable, as one may still see in the compositions of Unico Aretino, Antonio Tebaldeo, and some others; although their pieces are less disgusting than those of Sasso, Notturno, and Altissimo, they nevertheless show neither Dante's learning nor Petrarch's elegance.[24] Varchi's double censure—Unico's poetry was neither good nor unique in its badness—is most fully supported by D'Ancona, who ranks Accolti as one of the most mediocre imitators of Petrarch's wretched imitators and singles out his sonnet to an artichoke as an example of the depths to which these poets' bad taste sometimes sank.[25]

Whether we view *secentismo* in D'Ancona's terms, the "tumido e . . . pettoruto" style that flowered into Gongorism, or relate it to that lust for novelty Dr. Johnson scorned in the English Metaphysicals, or simply call it "baroque," it is a mannerism shared by Varchi's most and least "disgusting" poets. They all knew Petrarch by heart and relished the analogies he drew between subjective moods and objective phenomena. But there were elegant possibilities Petrarch had not fully exploited. So many arrows have pierced Tebaldeo's heart, for instance, that Cupid uses him as a quiver; the tears of his popular contemporary, Serafino, water the plains, relieving the thirsty cattle, but his sighs of unrequited passion scorch the birds passing above.[26] For the man Castiglione portrays as indulging "too much in extremes," the desire to turn tropes into facts and analogies into identities was just as irresistible. The best word to remember in passing from Accolti's theatrical life and lyrics to his one literal piece of theater, in fact, may be his characteristic "extremes": his melodramatic performances at the courts of popes and princes, his idealistic-cynical exhibitionism among the ladies, his choice of heroines as pure as the Blessed Virgin and as shameless as Helen, his fascination (in both his life and his lines) over love's power to exalt and destroy.

Even the *Virginia,* Accolti's only claim to greatness, is not entirely untraditional. From the standpoint of diction, it has a good number of *secentistico* passages, lengthy declamations that cultivate farfetched conceits at the temporary expense of dramatic interest. Also reflecting easily identifiable models are its basic plot, major characters, and method of construction, which is probably why recent critics are content to skirt the play with brief notes on its sources. For Mantovani, the *Virginia* is simply a comedy in *ottava rima* divided into five acts, whose plot is taken wholesale ("di peso") from Boccaccio but whose formal construction resembles that of the miracle play (I, 103). Santini is hardly more helpful when he comments that this adaptation of the *Decameron* and sacred drama projects some figures with contemporary appeal (I, 267). Even D'Ancona's three-page discussion of the play's central episodes[27] offers no hint of Accolti's originality. But with or without the heightening of *secentismo,* neither the heroine presented by Neifile nor the long-suffering ladies of sacred drama seem to suggest Wright's excessively astute, self-abasing groveler. As we have already noticed, the story of Giletta, that "savia donna," was clearly designed by the Queen as a sympathetic illustration of her own topic, a winsome example of "industria."[28] Similarly sympathetic, though not nearly so industrious or ingenious, are the often passive protagonists of the *sacre rappresentazioni,* Santa Guglielma, Stella, Rosana, and Santa Uliva, each a beautiful princess who endures all manner of persecution before being reunited with her beloved through the Blessed Virgin's intervention.

Perhaps one clue to Accolti's reason for first combining and then innovating upon these different traditions lies in his characteristic extremism. In dramatizing Boccaccio's brief narrative, he could have obliged classical tastes with more than a five-act structure. Except for a few low-comic scenes involving the Prince of Salerno's rascally servant, Ruffo, however, Accolti was not interested in the brisk dialogue and horseplay of Roman comedy. For the *secentismo* sonneteer, it was more natural to associate Giletta's travails with those of her spectacular sisters in the native dramatic tradition. Hence the *Virginia*'s disregard of the unities observed in contemporary learned comedy, its frequent and rapid shifts between Naples, Salerno, and Milan, its romantic insistence that time's passage be determined by each moment's emotive potential. Hence also its use of octaves not to describe events, as the *cantastorie* were doing in their songs about Roland, but primarily for characters to express their most personal feelings, as in the miracles.[29] Hence, finally, the *Virginia*'s huge cast of characters. As we might expect, almost every person Boccaccio even alludes to is given a speaking part. More important, however, is Accolti's addition of personae never mentioned by Boccaccio but included in at least three of the four miracle plays noted above: the royal couriers, a seneschal, councillors and chancellors, the heroine's mother (or stepmother). There is, in fact, only one major character common to all four plays yet absent from the *Virginia*, the Virgin herself, who always preserves her faithful daughter and usually effects as well a miraculous healing.[30]

In none of these solemn pieces, however, could a poet even as witty and cynical as Unico have found a suggestion of satire or irony, an encouragement to question the heroine's credentials. But the tale of Giletta, as we have noticed,[31] can be taken much less solemnly than its teller intended; read within the context Boccaccio manipulated, the other tales told on the Third Day, Neifile's celebration of a divinely sanctioned "industria" becomes an ironic part of a satirical whole that repeatedly unmasks religious rationalizations. The melodramatic, emotionally surcharged worlds of the miracle plays therefore offered Accolti much more than models for flights of *secentismo* and a method of constructing Giletta's adventures. They also furnished many elements Neifile had already represented as sublime and Dioneo as ridiculous: a pervasive theme of spiritual and physical healing, an atmosphere at once devoutly religious and extravagantly romantic, a tone affirming the values of sacred and profane love, and a strong trust in Providence.

Only an examination of the *Virginia* will reveal whether the playwright actually exploited the Dioncan perspective, but we may be fairly certain that he noticed and appreciated it. In the first place, Accolti must have been as familiar with Boccaccio's fiction as he was with Petrarch's poetry. Castiglione has his polite circle frequently couple these men as either the only models to imitate slavishly or the best examples to attempt to outdo (e.g., pp. 50, 61-62), and in the course of conversation the characters or events of at least nine scattered stories in the *Decameron* are casually alluded to, including one that shows what "a very great enemy of women" Boccaccio was, Ricciardo's bed-trick in III 6 (p. 193). Second, granting Accolti's familiarity with the tales surrounding Neifile's, the very roles he played to tease and flatter his sophisticated audiences indicate an intellect lively enough to have grasped Boccaccio's implications concerning disingenuous ingenuity, an ear quick to catch his mischievous refrain about that odd divinity which shapes our sexual ends.

Finally, if Accolti sought to dramatize Giletta's exploits in the spirit of his direct source's larger context, his heroine would have to become as unconventional and enigmatic as Wright apparently finds her. The *Virginia*'s importance, then, would not be based only upon its value in defining its tradition, the significance it assumed mainly by virtue of *All's Well,* but for its own high-comic achievements. Accolti was not the first to dramatize a *novella,* probably not even the first to borrow from the *Decameron.*[32] And for hints as to how the miracle play could be used to stage a profane tale, he could have turned to Poliziano's fairly recent *Orfeo* (1480), the first secular play in Italian, which replaces the angel-prologue with Mercury and Paradise with Olympus.[33] Accolti's originality would rather depend on how well he could realize Boccaccio's narrative relationships in dramatic terms, on finding theatrical equivalents for the interplay between tales and tellers like Dioneo's upending of Neifile's naive glosses.

Sensing the motive behind those bawdy, ethereal, and ironic responses to the announced topic's "industria" was, of course, a far simpler matter than finding a new way to convey the same point within a single staged piece. Unlike Accolti's low-comic scenes, which resemble earlier fifteenth-century imitations of Plautus and Terence, his main plot therefore employs a method of his own devising, less broad but wittier, a continuous and often whimsical alternation of scenes and sentiments sublime and mundane. Perhaps such a method was partly inspired by the *Decameron*'s juxtaposition of sexual and divine service; it also resembles the sentimental-cynical mask worn by Accolti, the courtier-poet extremist. But if the courts of the time offered numerous instances of the detached, high-comic spirit, its theaters rarely reflected anything approximating the spirit of high comedy. Back of the *Virginia* lay a century of Latin humanistic comedy, the sacred drama, the rustic *maggio,* but nothing like the deft exposures of social affectations and moral posturings that we find first in Accolti

and shortly thereafter in Ariosto, Bibbiena, Machiavelli, and Pietro
Aretino. Surely one measure of a writer's greatness, if not his uniqueness, is what he makes of materials on hand.

The first indication that the *Virginia* shares a Dionean perspective
appears in the Prologue's five-octave greeting. Neither Christian angel
nor pagan god, this courtly fellow both invokes and banishes commercial considerations, employs flattery only to comdemn it. Although
decrying "La voglia e sitial d'argento & oro, / Vil mercatura, ingrata
adulatione," for example, he assures his audience—nothing less than
"dei in carne humana"—that the play will show how "ardir, tempo,
ingegno, oro, & parole / Fanno ottcnere al fin cio che l'huom vuole"
(sigs. A2^r-A2^v). A similar juxtaposition of opposites occurs immediately thereafter with Virginia's entrance: a heroine whose name
suggests purity and innocence at once confesses to passions far stronger
than Giletta's and an ambition "horrenda impia & proterva"; a "semplice, & in esperta damigella" files a quasi-Petrarchan inventory of her
Prince's charms and "prove" that "havren forza a levar sua sposa a
Giove" (sigs. A3^r-A3^v).

Throughout the early scenes, in fact, Accolti continually strives for
such heightened, usually melodramatic effects. Through his heroine's
lengthy agonizing in *ottava rima,* her claim of being persecuted by
"ogni stella," and her association with physical healing—"Io d'Hippocrate fisico figliuola"—he encourages us to think of the miracle plays.
But these similarities between Virginia and the Virgin's faithful
daughters only make their great differences more noticeable. Whereas
they are sometimes the objects of other characters' illicit desires, sexual
passion here resides in the protagonist; whereas they are all of royal
blood, Virginia is socially far inferior to the man she craves and pursues,
the Prince of Salerno. If her admission "Che s'accenda del suo signor la
serva" reminds us of the *Decameron,* on the other hand, we should
realize that Accolti has ignored the less sensational aspects of Giletta's
situation: the wealthy young heiress rejecting each suitor proposed by
her guardians is now the isolated, distraught victim of a blind and
deadly passion—"tanto è cieco amor tanto è mortale / Ch'io vedo &
lodo el meglio, & seguo el peggio" (sig. A3^r). Even the Prologue's
passing reference to "Salernitana" seems designed to raise our expectations of the extraordinary. While Boccaccio's story contains no

characters that are remotely historical,[34] and while there is therefore
no special significance in Giletta's being from Nerbona, Virginia's
origin was a city so famous for its medical school that it was called
Civitas Hippocratica throughout Europe.[35]

For all Accolti's improvements on Boccaccio, however, the orginal
audience must have been at least as surprised by his improvement
upon recent history, political relationships that are first implied in
Virginia's relatively prosaic conclusion: "e sta mia stella / Col Rè
Alphonso in Parthenope bella" (sig. A3^v). We may be fairly certain that
most of the Sienese who watched the play in January, 1494, knew a
great deal about King Alphonso, the House of Aragon which had ruled
Parthenope or Naples since 1442, and the troubles it had experienced
with Ferrante Sanseverino, Prince of Salerno. When Alphonso I died in
1458, bequeathing the Kingdom of Naples to his bastard son, Ferdinand I, the most powerful of his barons declared for Ferdinand's
rival, John of Anjou, and only after six years of desolating warfare did
the son possess in fact what he had been left in theory.[36] And though
Ferdinand reigned for thirty-five years—he died toward the end of the
same month the *Virginia* was first performed—he was rarely at peace
with his proud nobles, especially the Sanseverini, the family that
usually headed the Angevin faction. The barons' most extensive up-
rising, what Benedetto Croce terms the "Great Conspiracy" of 1485-86,
was of course subsidized by the French court, where many of them fled
for refuge.[37] Their pleas that Charles VIII assert his claim to Naples
were eventually seconded by Lodovico Sforza, between whom and the
dukedom of Milan stood his nephew's Aragonese wife. Although the
French armies did not move south until August, 1494, most Italians
must have foreseen dark days for the House of Aragon earlier that year
when its old fox, Ferdinand, left the throne to his less talented son,
Alphonso II.

Given the repeated rebellions within and the proposed invasion from
without, any suggestion of Parthenope's political harmony must have
seemed as ironic as the news of the "Corriere adorno," who now
enters to announce that Alphonso's days may be numbered (sig. A3^v).
And as Accolti approaches the first of his play's grand confrontations,
Virginia's interview with the King, he continues to shape our responses
with ironic allusions. Learning of Alphonso's deadly fistula, Virginia

resolves "far del mio Principe acquisto" only after remembering the amorous achievements (but not the eventual miseries) of Ariadne, Semele, and Callisto. The scene now shifts to Naples, where the sickly Alphonso describes the vast regions of Parthenope, his possessions of whose "regno & thesor" is threatened only (so he believes) by his own malady (sig. A5^r). Finally, just before Virginia enters with her dual remedy ("Ch'al Re guarira el braccio, & a me el core"), the Prince ironically exhorts his liege to show wisdom in adversity, patience in sickness, and hope for a cure "Con arte, ingegno o vecchia esperientia" (sig. A5^r). "Ingegno" is the first word the Prologue uses to describe Virginia and one of the three words Virginia uses to describe what Love demands of his servants (sigs. A2^r, A4^v). And since we know that the heroine's "famoso licore" is a "vecchia esperientia"—with it her father once cured a queen's "fistola infetta"—we are prepared for an ingenious healing, a healthy King, and an afflicted Prince who is neither wise in adversity nor patient in "sickness."

But none of Accolti's melodramatic or ironic elaboration is quite so startling as his addition of an incident Boccaccio never even faintly suggests. We should recall that Giletta's entrance into the royal presence is described very matter-of-factly: "e appresso nel cospetto del re venuta, di grazia chiese che la sua infermità gli mostrasse" (I, 420). Since the king has already refused further medical attention, his granting of her request on the not very logical ground that she is "bella giovane e avvenente" indicates an amused, possibly skeptical point of view. In Accolti, however, the mischievous smile at an arbitrary French king becomes a cynical smirk at a vicious Neapolitan court. Among the "molta gente in questo loco" that Virginia now enters are two characters Accolti must have invented for the sake of mood and theme since they do nothing for the plot. The first is a surly guardsman who blocks her approach to Alphonso; the second is a gallant who comes to her aid: "Come prosumi o pien di vino & stolto / Voler tal donna a torto ingiuriare?" (sig. A6^r). Virginia's "pietoso volto" alone should move him, contends her champion, but the guardsman stands his ground: "Io non mi curo de le donne molto. / Che una gia mi stratiò." Compared to such thoughtless misogyny, the courtesy of this courtier— "servo di donne nato sono"—at first seems attractive. His introduction of her as a "gemma in oro, & fresco giglio in horto" apparently reflects the idealism of any "Giovin benigno," and even the solace he promises the King—"Ne veder la potrai senza conforto"—need not follow Boccaccio's sexual implications. It is rather in the King's response that we first find the source's comedy—"Se è bella, io son contento che la chiami"—as well as a new and sadder smile: "Ma guarda non sia quella che tu ami / Che rotta & fredda è stata tua proposta" (sig. A6^r). We hear no more about that unpleasant incident involving the young man's mistress, but enough has been said to undermine his gentility and to make us wonder about the health of the diseased King's court.

Virginia's greeting to Alphonso, "Te salvi el ciel," and her consequent explanation of what "al ciel cosi piacque" (sig. A6^v) once more supplant the cynical with the sublime, bringing us close to Neifile's self-appointed agent of the Almighty. But Giletta's claim that she heals "collo aiuto d'Iddio e colla scienzia del . . . mio padre" (I, 421) must be heightened to Virginia's "di mie prove / Tu stupirai in terra, & nel ciel Giove," and it is probably Accolti's own penchant for *secentismo* that makes his heroine appear smug or flippant rather than brave in the face of adversity. The King's threat to have her "membri adorni" burned if she fails is not weighed "una dramma"; she is, after all, already "nutrita di fiamma, esca di fiamma / . . . in terra elemento del foco" (sig. A7^r).

Within the week (whose passage is signified by eight "molto mi muove" octaves) we hear that the recovered King now "per dea l'adora" (sig. A8^v). Such adoration may point back to the source, the French king's willingness to test Giletta's divinity—"Forse m' è costei mandata da Dio" (I, 421)—and it certainly supports a reading of "pious" rather than merely "merciful" in the "fanciulla pia" (sig. Bl^r) by which the King now identifies his preserver. Quite ignorant of what the "ingegno grato" (cf. the Prologue's "mirabil ingegno") of the King's goddess has contrived, the Prince enters with a wish for heaven's direction—"Te salvi o Re el ciel sommo & superno"—but he is shortly railing against "questa donna, che con falsità" and "inganno" vanquished his will and hoping that he may "l' ingannatrice inganni" (sig. B3^r-B3^v). But Virginia is not the only party responsible for the Prince's bitter redefining of "ingegno" as "inganno." Like Boccaccio's arbitrary sovereign, not to mention Shakespeare's, Alphonso would remain true to his bargain at another's expense. None of the "giustitia, & . . . pietate" he directs the Prince to rule by is found in his own sudden display of power, and his own naive conclusion that this festive night "veramente è felice & serena" (sig. B2^v) seems to represent Accolti's way of deceiving the deceiver.

Another means Accolti employs to relate "ignanno" and "ingegno" are the escapades of the Prince's wily servant, Ruffo, a scrambling, snatching, bullying, thieving pander—everything, in short, that the modern *ruffa, raffa, riffa,* and *ruffiano* suggest and quite close to John Florio's sense of *rúffo,* "a ruffian, a swagrer, or a ruffling roister."[38] Partly the classsical parasite, partly the clever slave and braggart soldier, Ruffo devotes his wicked wit and boundless energy to lusting after or theologizing over womankind, created by the devil when God was out for a stroll ("Quando nacquero il Dio andava a spasso / Et credo la facessi sathanasso," sig. B6^r). At first confident that neither the Prince's love, Camilla, nor her mother, Costanza, is a match for his "ingegno & arte"—"preci pie," "volto di Marte," "molte bugie"—he soon concludes that plain gold works better than the fanciest fictions: "Frappa se sai," he cautions, "Senza oro non farai cosa che vogli" (sig. Cl^v). Even his most sincere pose—hair combed, face shaved, stomach corseted, thick kips sucked in and eyes overflowing with what will pass for tears, his own saliva—does not impress constant Costanza, that "Vecchia ribalda d'antichristo madre" (sig. C2^r).

But the clearest evidence of Accolti's desire to puncture social pretensions by mingling the ethereal and earthly lies in his having the play's most idealistic sentiments, the Prince's love letter to Camilla, declaimed by its dirtiest character. For ninety-seven lines it is Ruffo who weeps and wastes away, whose soul burns, who protests that "in nobil cor mai non alberga inganno" (sig. Cl^r). Given Ruffo's self-serving nature, we are not surprised to see him open and read the letter his master entrusts him with. Since Accolti has him read it *aloud* (when it would have been as easy and surely more romantic first to let the Prince himself rehearse his Petrarchan passion and then allow the cynical servant to scan the lines silently), it appears that irony is controlling melodrama and *secentismo* being forced to fuel comedy.

Even as Accolti allows Ruffo to ridicule the sublime, another amorous epistle, no less farfetched, is delivered by the Salernese chancellors, Callimaco and Domitio, who beg the Prince's hearing "perche tutte le gratie divine / Ti conceda el signor del sommo chiostro" (sig. C3^v).

Because Salerno agrees only to hear Domitio read Virginia's letter, not to peruse it himself, the play's second passionate address, like the first, must be declaimed by a third party. The petition itself is remakable not for its conventional anguish—the left hand holding "ferro, & veneno" while the right falters with a pen dipped in "lagrime & sangue"—but for its curious reasoning, the rhetoric with which Virginia moves from self-condemnation to self-justification, from "mio fallo insano / E . . . tuo giusto sdegno" in the opening lines to her closing concession, "Ben ch'a torto da te stratiata sia, / Non cerco el morir tuo" (sigs. C3ᵛ-C5ᵛ). It is impossible to pinpoint where "ingegno" becomes purely "inganno," but by tercets ten through thirteen we are reminded of Wright's comments concerning Virginia's astute self-abasement as well as of Boccaccio's exposure of religious rationalizing.

> Che dove offender puoi è gran vendetta,
>   El perdonare, ch'a ogni humano eccesso
>   Non lascia sempre Giove ir sua saetta:
> A piedi tuoi mi stendo, & io confesso
>   Essere incolpa, riguarda al Leone
>   Che non è crudo a l'huom ch'è genuflesso:
> Habbi di me qualche compassione,
>   Pietà mi impetri l'infinito amore
>   Che merta gratia & non desperatione.
> Che s'io errai, ha purgato ogni errore
>   La stanca faccia di lagrime piena,
>   Ed ogni pena è vinta dal dolore. [Sigs. C4ʳ-C4ᵛ]

Since Virginia has sinned, the Prince is obliged to follow the examples of the kings of gods and beasts; *if* she has sinned, her own suffering obviates the need for such forgiveness. And between these contradictory assertions is an equally illogical mercy that obtains a love that *merits grace.*

But the Prince only scorns "tanto inganno," even after Callimaco insists "cha'ngannarti la constrinse amore" (sig. C5ᵛ). The "dura impossibil conditione" he immediately sets bespeak Boccaccio's plot, but the ironies developed in the next few episodes indicate just as surely the Dionean perspective. At first Accolti apparently strives to elicit sympathy for his heroine: Domitio has "gran compassione" for this lady; Callimaco calls the Prince "crudo, et pien d'orgoglio"; Virginia, quite "innocente," calls on Death, and her maids rush about to relieve "queste membra tribolate & frante" (sigs. C6ʳ-C6ᵛ). The same pathos characterizes Virginia's eighty-line farewell to her subjects, during which she forgives Salerno for "l'immerite doglie, / El morir mio d'ogni ingiustitia pieno," and vows to spend her last moments wandering in the wilderness, "Poi che non piace al ciel ch'io sia felice" (sig. C7ᵛ-C8ʳ). But no sooner have her tearful subjects departed than she shatters this sublime mood (and what she professed to be Heaven's will) with the frankest of confessions: "Sol per venir del mio disegno al fine / Celato ho el vero," the truth of making straightway for Milan and "le bellezze divine / Del Principe" (sig. C8ᵛ).

In emphasizing the heroines' attention to appearances—the word "honesto" is used three times in one stanza—Accolti is merely following his source ("honesto" is one of Neifile' favorite words; see I, 425-28, where she uses it or "onestamente" or "onestissima" five times). But Giletta's shifts take shape slowly, calmly, and methodically, whereas Accolti prefers to startle his audience, using every possible melodramatic device to convince us of Virginia's helplessness before abruptly revealing her strength. And though she is more often offstage than on during the rest of the play, we are never allowed to forget that she is directing the action, seducing the would-be seducer with plots beyond the depth of his designing servant. To enforce the irony of the pursuer pursued, Accolti has one party unknowingly echo or describe another. "Andiamo," cries Virginia, hurrying her maids off to Sabina's inn; "Andiam," cries the Prince in the very next line, as he hurries Ruffo back to Camilla's (sig. D1ʳ). Although Ruffo knows much about the game of love—"Scaccian chi viene & chiaman quel che fugge / Queste donne"—he is woefully ignorant of its most important player.

Far most subtle and clear-sighted is Ruffo's chief adversary, the widow Costanza, whose moral-commercial dialogues with Virginia add a mischievous note found not in Neifile's story but in the tales that surround it. Having heard from Sabina of the Prince's passion for Camilla, Virginia immediately (and characteristically) senses some higher power at work: "Forse dopo un mio lungo lagrimare / Sarò da qualche stella pia riscossa" (sig. D1ᵛ). This compassionate star, however, requires that Costanza be "prudente" as well as "casta" and a

"poveretta," for "la forza dell'or troppo è possente." Virginia's overtures naturally ignore such prudent concerns, though the bed-trick is
introduced as a means of employing "prudentia e ingegno" (sig. D2ᵛ).
The widow is rather asked to accept the heroine's shaping divinity:
"Et co'l Principe me come el ciel mostra / Poniate in cambio della
figlia vostra." Although understandably anxious about her reputation,
Costanza eventually skirts another issue, something akin to Virginia's
earlier reflection on the power of gold: "Chi va a l'util dietro non
s'accorge / Che in un continuo mal tale util torna" (sig. D3ʳ).

Just as Sabina said nothing to encourage Virginia's faith in Costanza's
prudence, so Virginia has said nothing to inspire Costanza's comments
on those who pursue profit. Virginia replies in kind, however, with a
model of euphemistic casuistry, first allaying Costanza's explicit fears
by promising that "Quando si sappi un si piatoso inganno / Ne sarai
commendata in infinito," then acknowledging the "util" she hinted at by
repeatedly promising a handsome dowry for Camilla, and finally
glancing darkly at the risks "Se tua figlia non sposi presto & bene"
(sig. D3ᵛ). Dioneo could not have done a wittier job of questioning
Neifile's earnest efforts to sanctify deceit. Following so many narrators
who have stressed hypocritical means to selfish ends, it behooves the
Queen to emphasize how "la gentil donna" desires nothing more than
"consolarsi onestamente"; "avendo l'animo gentil," the woman need
only be convinced that her role in the assignation would be an "onesta
cosa" leading to an "onesto fine" (I, 426-28). But the lady-narrator
doth protest too much her characters' innocence, and the smiles
Boccaccio encourages probably influenced Accolti's repeated use of
euphemisms.

Another method Neifile employs to idealize her heroine's trickery
may have suggested some of the *Virginia*'s most humorous low-comic
scenes. To make her agent's part in the bed-trick more palatable,
Giletta offers a pious hope that "Forse mi farà Iddio grazia d'ingravidare" (I, 428). This wish is of course Neifile's first move in sealing her
heroine's program with God's approval; in the next paragraph we are
offered a sign few would dare gainsay: "Ne' quali primi congiugnimenti
. . . come fu piacer di Dio, la donna ingravidò." But blocking Nefile's
path is Boccaccio's own ironic interplay. Signs of surety have been and
will continue to be whimsically questioned by the Third Day's other

storytellers, and it appears that Accolti honors that quizzical spirit with the largely farcical doings of Ruffo and his befuddled master in the rest of Act III. Since Virginia has instructed Costanza to show Ruffo a "faccia pia" (sig. D3ᵛ), the bully's third attempt is welcomed with a smile. Still suspicious, he is nevertheless comforted by this omen of success: "Che Volpe è questa vitiata & maestra / Pur è buon segno haver da lei buon viso." And though Ruffo now prefers to keep God out of the picture—to Costanza's "El cielo salvi e pensier tuoi" he replies, "Tu sola, non el ciel salvar mi puoi" (sig. D4ᵛ)—he is soon congratulating himself for his success: "Questa novella al mio signore arreco, / Che dormira con lei, & io con teco?

The most ludicrous part of this interview, however, are the details of so ironic a tryst, procedures odd in their own right and in being devised and discussed with such apparent seriousness. The Prince must arrive "a cinque hore, / Batti le palme, & venga senza gente, / Aspetti d'acqua ch'io versi el romore" (sig. D5ʳ). Possessing such valuable information enables Ruffo to lord it over his proud master—"intendo . . ./ Schernirlo alquanto essermi vendicato"—but the teasing subsides before the instructions are given, even though the Prince is now evidently to feel as well as to hear the water: "Che per segno acqua a te gettata fia" (sig. D5ᵛ). Was water actually thrown upon or merely toward the Prince? His first response, "Sentito ho l'acqua" (sig. D7ʳ), does not tell us what the audience saw. Neither does his subsequent moralization: "Poca acqua è questa a spegnere el mio foco." Another unanswerable question is what associations Accolti's audience made with this strange sign. Ruffo tells the Prince that if Camilla knew of his reluctance to surrender the ring, "Non ti laveria l'acqua del Danubbio" (sig. D6ʳ). Perhaps the water Costanza pours out also represented some cleansing ritual, the lover's baptism. But if "a cinque hore" refers to the fifth hour after sunset, it is just as possible that the audience thought of another ritual, pouring out the slops at curfew.

In any case, earthly and heavenly considerations continue to alternate in the short scenes that conclude Act III and initiate Act IV. To herself Costanza confesses being motivated by both "Tanta pietà di questa donna" and "la dota ch'io guadagno scorto" (sig. D6ᵛ). Virginia then enters to thank her "pia, piatosa, & chara" servant: "In prima Dio ringratio & te da poi." The next stanza ushers in the Prince, the happiest

person "sotto el ciel" and ironically grateful: "Io ti ringratio benigna
fortuna" (sig. D7^r). But he is immediately replaced by Costanza, pray-
ing "el ciel non si scopra l'inganno," and he returns only to describe the
joys he thinks he has just experienced with Camilla. Still wiser than he
realizes, Ruffo closes Act III with a question for the audience, "Fidate
poi di queste donne ladre," and Virginia and Costanza open Act IV
with the same sublime-mundane considerations that characterized their
initial bargaining. Having fulfilled the impossible conditions "Per la
Dio gratia & tua," Virginia bids her agent fix her own reward. To the
very same request Neifile's "gentil donna" simply answers that she has
not done a thing "per alcuna speranza di guiderdone, ma perché le
pareva doverlo fare a voler ben fare" (I, 429). Costanza is even more
"gentil" and therefore even less direct. She requires half a stanza only
to express her joy in serving the "generosa" princess and another half to
ask for nothing and hint for much:

> Nulla ti chiederei donna pietosa
> Sol di tua gratia resto, & son contenta,
> Che a cor gentil son parole proterve,
> Et chiede assai chi ben tacendo serve. [Sig. D8^r]

It is these problematical sentiments and ironies never hinted at by
Neifile that remind us most of Boccaccio's framework and, for that
matter, of the darker corners of Shakespeare's comedy. Accolti's own
respresentation of "our life['s] . . . mingled yarn" allows Ruffo a
sudden Parolles-like self-knowledge ("A me sta ben se ogni vitio osservo,
/ Che ignobil son plebeo, povero & servo") as well as some ironic moralizing, "El fin mostra, [c]hi ha piu senno fido" (sigs. E2^r, E3^v). The
Prince's melodramatic mourning for the loss of a woman he actually
shunned sounds another ironic note. So does Callimaco's "Gratia habbi
el ciel, poi che ti ci ha renduto," if we remember Virginia's role as
heaven's agent. The theme of divine direction is most clearly and ironically sounded at the climax when the Prince, pitying the dejected lady
before him, swears "per quello immortale / Che'n cielo e'n terra ha
somma monarchia" that "ogni gratia da me fatta ti fia / Se ben
m'havessi offesso" (sig. E8^r). Within this religious context Virginia
expands and contracts the magnitude of her guilt to suit the changing
directions of her theme. The Prince was rightly offended by what Love

compelled her to do, yet he should easily forgive what was engineered "con pietoso inganno" (sig. Fl^v). Whether "pietoso" is here taken as "piteous" or "pious." the "inganno" is defended with the heroine's customary "ingegno"—139 lines of sweeping rhetoric that culminate in her offering her breast to his blade, provided, of course, that he later open up her heart to find his name inscribed (sig. F2^r).

True to his course throughout the play, however, Accolti is more skeptical as well as more sentimental than Neifile. When her two-line, matter-of-fact comment concerning Beltramo's return to Rossiglione is inflated into Salerno's twenty-four-line agonizing, we almost expect to find the speaker's sincerity—"Ruffo io son disperato, anzi son morto"—eventually qualified by his ignorance—"Se visto havessi el corpo peregrino" (sig. El^r). The same technique of exaggerating only to undercut is found in the nine impassioned ocataves that conclude Act IV. Silvio, created out of nothing more than Neifile's passing reference to Giletta's suitors (I, 419), laments his beloved's imminent death for lack of sufficient "forza, o ingegno" and vows to undertake "ogni impossibil cosa" to find her, first questing among the conventional "selve, & fere impaste" and then through places and times increasingly removed, from a realistic "Danubio veloce" to an exotic "Eufrate che l'arene coce," from "le selve nude" of the ancient Parthians to the never-existing "sette Insule pie" and, just for good measure, "e sette crude." There is a similarly facetious tone behind the expansive geo-graphy of Act V as the Seneschal, turning Neifile's brief notice of Beltramo's "gran festa" (I, 430) into fifty-two lines of unrelieved hyperbole, bids the Prince's hunters bring back an eagle, a griffin, a phoenix, and the fishermen, everything from oysters to whales—"Et se possibil fusse una serena" (sig. E6^v).

In Virginia's extravagant summation of her sorrows before the Salernese nobility we find the same uneasy balance between high seriousness and high comedy. While the befuddled hero speaks more and more ironically—directing his Seneschal, for example, "Non lasciar cosa entrar che ci dispiaccia"—the clear-eyed heroine publicly maintains her innocence and privately admits her cunning. To Sabina she explains that the "stelle fortuna, & fata humano. / M'hanno arrichita di doppio figliuolo," but she next addresses the babes themselves as precious things "Acquistati da me con tanto ingegno" (sigs. E7^r-E7^v).

To her husband and his court, however, it is mainly a matter of making "ingegno" look "piatoso." The Prince's "per quello immortale" therefore becomes "Per quel sommo fattor, ch'el tutto vede" and is joined to "Per le cener del tuo pio genitore" and "Per mio fervente & infinito amore" (sig. F1ᵛ). Such parallelisms support the "logic" of Virginia's claim: the mercy that family honor or tradition encourages is the mercy that God upholds and her own love deserves. But if such grand theater outdoes Neifile's melodramatic resolution—Accolti turns the weeping heroine into the weeping everyone (sig. F3ʳ)—it also seems to question its credibility, transforming the husband who loves so suddenly and unreservedly into a weary actor feeling out various roles to meet an astonishing turn of events: the good sportsman grudgingly admiring such "inaudito estremo ingegno," the good ruler bending to his subjects' wishes, the proud man trying to become magnanimous and, finally, the husband humbled before heaven's will (or comic conventions): "Andiamo poi ch' el ciel qui te compiace / Di quel ch'a me non creder gia che annoglia" (sig. F3ᵛ).

The concluding comment on all ending well, however, comes in the Seneschal's three-octave epilogue. For the man who has done so much ordering and arranging during the last two acts there is a natural reluctance to extend the festivities; hence, the play's final joke—each spectator is invited to dine in his own house. But for this loyal servant there is no question of the couple's future happiness or of the play's moral import: the fact that Virginia, "Per suo ingegno, & virtu," has achieved her desires is proof that

> il meritato premio al fin raccoglie
> Ciascun, de l'opra sua, o bona, o fella
> Che cosi da d'Iddio le giuste voglie. [Sig. F4ʳ]

Like Neifile, the Seneschal is prone to gloss over minor problems: the frequent coupling of "ingegno" and "inganno," a "virtu" that is more efficient than virtuous. Notice, too, that his conviction that all must be well is based not on what has happened but on his notion of what God's just will must grant or allow, a faith in a perfectly ordered, poetically just universe that is both unrealistic and un-Christian. What supports his faith is precisely what supports Neifile's, a clever heroine who has dressed God's just will to her own advantage. The playwright

whose own performances before princes and popes made him ideally
suited to expand upon the meaning of Giletta's ingenious deceits
seems to be reminding us again that Boccaccio's allegedly simple virtue
story is fraught with affectations and ironies.

Even in its closing moments, then, the *Virginia* reveals its intrinsic
worth as sustained high comedy as well as its value in interpreting the
great art is based upon. But of what use is Accolti's neglected play
in glossing the greatest "chapter" of the *All's Well* story? Although a
definitive answer to this question must be postponed until we have
examined later potential influences upon Shakespeare, here we may at
least notice that Virginia encourages us to approach Helena with
Giletta's dubious piety in mind. Together, these early Renaissance
heroines give us not only a common theme to look for in Shakespeare
but an assurance that an ironic or cynical treatment of that theme is
not necessarily anachronistic. As we turn to Helena's sixteenth- and
early-seventeenth-century sisters, we must also allow for a latter-day
Countess of Artois. But given the surprising popularity of the *Virginia*
and the obscurity of *Le Chevalereux Comte d'Artois,*[39] at this point
Italian mischief would seem a likelier influence than Burgundian idealism.

NOTES

1. An undated letter, cited by Giammaria Mazzuchelli, *Gli Scrittori D'Italia,* I, 66.

2. Ralph Roeder, *The Man of the Renaissance,* p. 318.

3. Francesco De Santis, *History of Italian Literature,* I, 432.

4. *Orlando Furioso,* ed. Lanfranco Caretti, XLVI, 14.

5. Roeder, p. 532.

6. See, for example, Corrado Lazzeri, "Arezzo," *Enciclopedia Italiana,* IV, 171.

7. Caccio da Narni, *Morte del Danese* (1521), II, iv, 126 as cited in Mazzuchelli, I, 67, n. 12.

8. Alessandro D'Ancona, *Studi sulla Letteratura Italiana de' Primi Secoli,* pp. 151-237, esp. p. 218.

9. See pp. 4-5.

10. *Boccaccio in England from Chaucer to Tennyson,* pp. 215-16.

11. "Accolti, Bernardo," *Enciclopedia Italiana,* I, 267. Cf. Lilia Mantovani's biographical comments in *Dizionario Biografico degli Italiani,* I, 103-4.

12. Mantovani, I, 103; also see Mazzuchelli, I, 66.

13. Mantovani, I, 103.

14. *Verginia,* sig. F5ʳ. All citations to Accolti's work are to the edition printed for Zoppino (Venice, 1535), which probably appeared shortly after his death on 1 March of that year. See n. 39 below.

15. See Montovani, I, 103.

16. Ibid.

17. Mazzuchelli, I, 66-67. Alfonso did not succeed his father as Duke of Nepi according to Mantovani, I, 104, and Girolamo Tiraboschi, *Storia della Letteratura Italiana,* III, 164.

18. Cf. Mazzuchelli, I, 67; Santini, I, 267; Mantovani, I, 103.

19. Mantovani, I, 103.

20. This letter of April, 1516, is cited by Tiraboschi, III, 164.

21. Mantovani, I, 103.

22. E.g., Santini, I, 267 and D'Ancona, *Studi,* pp. 216-18.

23. *The Courtier,* trans. Charles S. Singleton, p. 17.

24. From the *Ercolano* (1580), as cited by Mazzuchelli, I, 67, n. 10.

25. *Studi,* p. 218.

26. See Jefferson Butler Fletcher, *Literature of the Italian Renaissance,* pp. 220-22, and Ernest Hatch Wilkins, *A History of Italian Literature,* rev. Thomas G. Bergin, pp. 174-76.

27. Alessandro D'Ancona, *Origini del Teatro Italiano,* II, 15-17.

28. *Decameron,* ed. Vittore Branca, I, 308. Branca, whose edition is cited throughout this chapter, glosses "industria" as "ingegnosità, abilità."

29. Accolti's only departures from the octave are three lengthy passages in *terza rima,* exceptions that only confirm the rule about his penchant for melodrama: the Prince's passionate love letter to Camilla (97 lines); Virginia's anguished petition to her husband (112 lines); Virginia's extravagant summation of her sorrows before the Salernese nobility (139 lines).

30. Two of Burgundy's wisest doctors cure Stella's wounds, but her amputated hands are only later restored by the Virgin; Uliva's mutilated members are similarly recovered; Guglielma assumes the Virgin's role when she cures a Hungarian prince of a leprosy beyond his physician's practice. See *Sacre Rappresentazioni del Quattrocento,* ed. Luigi Banfi, pp. 565 ff., 602 ff., 634, 770. The Virgin does not appear in *La Rappresentazione di Rosana,* but an angel enters to tell the heroine that the Mother of God has heard her prayers and will grant them (p. 707).

31. See pp. 20 ff.

32. See Vittorio Rossi, *Il Quattrocento,* rev. Aldo Vallone, pp. 502, 508, and Madeleine Doran, *Endeavors of Art: A Study of Form in Elizabethan Drama,* pp. 103, 191.

33. Joseph Spencer Kennard, *The Italian Theatre,* I, 89, 158; cf. Wilkins, p. 154.

34. Branca, I, 419, n. 2.

35. Kennard, I, 95; Wright, p. 187.

36. Alfred de Reumont, *The Carafas of Maddaloni: Naples under Spanish Dominion,* pp. 6-7.

37. Benedetto Croce, *History of the Kingdom of Naples*, p. 92.

38. *Queen Anna's New World of Words*, p. 455.

39. Mazzuchelli, I, 67-68, lists six editions of the *Virginia:* 1513, 1515, 1519, 1553, 1565, 1586; to these we should add our text (Venice, 1535), first noticed by Enrico Narducci, *Atti della R. Accademia dei Lincei, XII*, XII, 6; an eighth edition (Florence, 1518) not noted by either bibliographer is found in the University of Illinois Library. Until Barrois collated, edited, and published *Le Chevalereux Comte d'Artois* in 1837, it existed in two fairly similar and relatively unknown manuscripts; see Barrois, pp. ix-xiv.

V

Boccacio Translated and Transfigured: Le Maçon, Ruscelli, Painter, Salviati, and Florio

One Girolamo Ruscelli, a learned Italyan making prety notes for the better elucidation of the Italyan Decamerone of Boccaccio, judgeth Boccaccio himselfe to be this schollar, whom by an other name he termeth to be Rinieri. But whatsoever that Scholler was, he was truely to extreme in reveng, and therein could use no meane.

William Painter, *The Second Tome of the Palace of Pleasure*

If the *Decameron* encourages several different readings of the *All's Well* story—Neifile's, Dioneo's, Boccaccio's—so do its sixteenth-century editors and translators, whose "prety notes" and wholesale expurgations usually obscure the dramatic interplay of the artist they sought to honor. Evidently offending neither moral nor ecclesiastical sensibilities, the tale of Giletta long escaped the "better elucidation" to which the rest of the Third Day's stories were subjected. Not until the first complete English translation of 1620, probably by John Florio, do we find Neifile's narrative significantly altered. But through the second half of the sixteenth century the concerns that led Florio to obliterate Boccaccio's design, and thereby the most viable meaning of III 9, become increasingly clear. Like honest Master Painter, moreover, many commentators, including Florio, seem to have been inspired by their predecessors' learning only to wander even farther from the spirit of the stories they so conscientiously glossed.

One of the earliest (and therefore most faithful) of the seventy-seven sixteenth-century editions of the *Decameron*[1] is that of Niccolò Delfino (Venice, 1516). Its astonishingly plain title, *Del Decamerone di M. Giovanni Boccaccio,* is a fitting introduction to its elegant simplicity: no dedicatory epistles to important people, merely a one-page request that all "gentili et valorose donne . . . hora con lieto volto leggete, & rileggete il vostro non mai bastevolmente lodato Decamerone"; none of the extensive "dichiarationi, annotiationi, et avvertimenti" that become so common by the middle of the century, only a three-page list of printer's errors. Unlike his successors, Delfino evidently assumed that the *Decameron* needed editorial adornments no more than expurgations.

Remarkably different assumptions underlie Gabriel Giolito's edition, published in Venice exactly thirty years later, which takes nothing away from Boccaccio but adds a great deal. A concern for the needs of the "studiosi della lingua volgare" is registered both in the 64-word title and in Giolito's prefatory comments. To that scholarly end, Giolito furnishes a running marginal commentary and concludes his edition with Francesco Sansovino's "Dichiaratione di tutti i vocabili . . . e luoghi difficili." Unfortunately, both men's scholarship is almost exclusively philological. The closest we get to a literary gloss of the Third Day's tales is Sansovino's wholly humorless explication of Boccaccio's description of monna Isabetta "forse cavalcando allora senza sella la bestia di . . . san Giovanni Gualberto" (III 4): "San Giovanni Gualberto," he explains, "è una chiesa in Firenze," and this leads him to a lengthy discussion of how its founder came to be sainted (sigs. Civ^v-Cvi^v). Much more misleading than this patently irrelevant stuff, however, are the moral comments that immediately follow (and appear to enjoy the same authority as) the tales' headnotes. Boccaccio's epitome of Masetto's frolic with the nuns (III 1), for example, is left intact, but we are at once told what the story really means: "Nel che si contiene, quanto sia difficil cosa a serbare in tutti i luoghi la virginità" (sig. Hviii^r). Similarly, Alibech's sexual-religious enlightenment (III 10) allegedly illustrates how easy it is for one driven by "li stimoli della carne . . . sotto ombra di religione ingannare una semplice & sciocca femina" (sig. Mi^r). And there is, of course, no suggestion that the Queen's story has anything in common with its successor's sexually motivated deception: "Nel che si loda principalmente l'ingegno & il senno delle valorose donne" (sig. Lvi^r).

What saved the *Decameron* from further moral incursions were not the Italian scholars and publishers, increasingly pressured by the Council of Trent (1545-63), so much as the thoroughly congenial and highly influential translation of Antoine le Maçon, the first of whose eighteen sixteenth-century editions[2] was published in Paris the very year the Council began sitting. This French Bocaccio was never expurgated, "corrected" or, except for one interval (1580-96), long silenced. While "la malvagità de' cherici" disappeared in Venice and Florence, "la mechanceté des gens d'eglise" burgeoned in Paris, Lyons, and Rotterdam. At every turn le Maçon's racy narrative justifies the claim of the commendatory "Dixain aux Lecteurs" that

> Bocace est icy mieux recongneu,
> Que si luy mesme, à se faire escouter,
> Fust de Florence en France revenu.[3]

For six years the French *Decameron* even resisted Giolito's moral appendages. They appear neither in the first two editions (Paris, 1545, 1548), printed under le Maçon's personal direction, nor in several succeeding Parisian editions (1551, 1554, 1556), but in the first Lyons edition of 1551, printed by Guillaume Rouillé, and in all other sixteenth-century versions.[4] Whether Rouillé was looking back to Laurent de Premierfait's notion of the *Decameron* as a handbook of precepts or forward to the resolutions at Trent, it took little skill to Gallicize the morals he probably found in Giolito. Compare, for example, the Italian meaning of III 1 with "Souz laquelle est monstré qu'il est bien difficile à garder la virginité en tous lieux." By 1555, an Italian edition printed in Lyons by "Gulielmo Rovillio" adds these flourishes: "Nel che si contiene, quanto sia difficil cosa alle donne il serbare non pure ne luoghi profani, ma ancho ne monasteri, la virginità." Similarly, the virtues III 9 supposedly celebrate are now inflated into "non meno la castita, che il senno, l'avedimento & la costanza delle savie & valorose Donne," and Rouillé drives the point home by foisting this couplet upon Boccaccio's conclusion: "Vince l' humanità il cor altiero, / Se con sagacità seguita il vero" (sig. Vvi^v).

Even through the 1550s, however, some reasonably faithful Venetian editions of the *Decameron* were still appearing. In 1557 Francesco Alunno offered an unmoralized, unexpurgated text, prefixed only by a now customary "Tavola" and a dedicatory epistle celebrating Boccaccio's work as the principal basis of the Tuscan tongue. Equally faithful but far more ambitious was the edition of Girolamo Ruscelli (Venice, 1552), which clearly distinguishes between textual facts and editorial opinions. In his letter to the reader (sigs. vi^r-vi^v), Ruscelli mentions Giolito's having published Boccaccio eight to ten times; it is to his credit that he ignores Giolito's unauthoritative morals while attempting to rival his annotations. Like Giolito's, his interests are primarily philological and grammatical; one could hardly infer from his marginal commentaries that the contents of III 9 and III 10 are quite different. The lengthy "Annotationi" at the end of the Third Day focus exclusively on three troublesome verbs, and the "prety notes" Painter mentions are, from a literary standpoint, quite rare. Ruscelli is much like the unruffled gentleman who remarks upon the bad grammar of obscene graffiti. His gloss of the punch line of II 10 ("Il mal furo [thief] non vuol festa"), for example, is an unblushing "Foro, pertugio, & si legge con la .o. stretta come honoro" (sig. Hiii^v). Would that Ruscelli's annotations evidenced as clearly an understanding of Boccaccio's larger designs.

As an Englishman of the 1560s, William Painter found it far more difficult to remain morally distanced from his matter. The full titles of both tomes of *The Palace of Pleasure* (London, 1566, 1567) claim that what follows has been "selected out of divers good and commedable Authors," and in the dedicatory epistle to the first tome Painter assures us that only the most edifying parts of those good authors have passed inspection, for example either "the vertuous mindes of noble Dames, the chaste hartes of constant Ladyes, . . . the mild sufferaunce of well disposed gentlewomen" or "the uglye shapes of insolencye and pride, the deforme figures of incontinencie" and "deceitfull devises."[5] But in the case of Boccaccio, Painter later admits to the general reader, only a small portion can be salvaged even under the relatively liberal policy of "the best to be followed, and the worst to be avoyded." "There be some (in my judgement) that be worthy to be comdempned to perpetual prison," he admits, "but of them such have I redeemed . . . as may be best liked, and better suffered. Although the sixt part of the same hundreth may full well be permitted."[6]

It is unfortunate that Painter did not save III 9 for his second tome, wherein all but three of his thirty-five stories receive specific moral comments (II, 154-57). Judging from his claim that "Boccaccio for his stile, order of writing, gravitie, and sententious discourse, is worthy of intire provulgation" and his emphasis upon poetic justice in the score of tales he alludes to in the introduction to his first tome (I, 11-13), Painter probably thought—and certainly could have easily proved—that Giletta also exemplified "the best to be followed." Still, there are some indications that this first English teller of the *All's Well* story was not wholly comfortable with it. First, while moralizing over almost two dozen protagonists, including models of chastity, fidelity and "base birth . . . advaunced (by fortune's grace) to highe estate," he passes over Giletta without comment. Next, after consecutively drawing upon three stories in the First Day and five in the Second, Painter could find only one suitable tale in the Third. Would not this day's pervasive bawdy have led him to question the *Decameron*'s method?

In his second tome Painter reveals some understanding of Boccaccio's design. The four tales he took from the Tenth Day (which celebrates magnanimity) are introduced collectively: "Mistresse Dianora, Mithridanes and Nathan, Katherine of Bologna, and Saladine, the mutual curtesies of noble and gentle Personages" (II, 155). But Painter also shows that he can ignore Boccaccio's directions. The *Decameron* is quite clear that the Eighth Day deals with tricks men and women play upon one another, and the headnote to the seventh story sounds the theme of measure for measure. Painter nonetheless introduces this story as evidence of "what lothsom lustes do lurk under the bark of fading beauty, what stench of filthy affection fumeth from the smoldring gulfe of dishonest Love, what prankes such dames do play for deceit of other, and shame of themselves" (II, 156). Surely Painter realized that such high seriousness was as far from Boccaccio's *beffe* as the lengthy misogynistic opening of his "translation" (III, 329-30) was from the Italian and French texts before him. With Ruscelli "at his elbow" and le Maçon as "his mainstay,"[7] Painter makes only one significant error in translating III 9: he turns Neifile's conditional clause, "come il parto al suo tempo venuto fece manifesto" (cf. le

Maçon's "ainsi que son enfantement (quand le temps en fut venu) en rendit certaine asseurance") into a simple conjunctive, "and her delivery chaunced at the due time," thus obscuring the Queen's implication that the precise time of Giletta's delivery indirectly established God's help in her bed-plot. Stripped of the context Boccaccio had furnished, however, even this relatively accurate version of the *All's Well* story was bound to be misleading.

Not long after Painter had reconciled one-sixth of the *Decameron* to Protestant morality, several Florentine men of letters, deputized by the Inquisition and headed by Vincenzo Borghini, forced the whole work into agreement with Catholic discipline. Although published in Boccaccio's native Florence (1573) and edited by his own countrymen, the title makes no bones about this *Decameron* having been "Ricorretto in Roma, et Emendato secondo l'ordine del Sacro Conc. di Trento." And though the epistle dedicatory laments Boccaccio's having spoken in jest things that seem "meno che convenevoli a grave huomo, & di Christiana religione professore," it soon becomes clear that his offenses were less moral than ecclesiastical. Borghini does not touch the *Tavola*'s headnotes to I, 1, 3, 5, 7-10 and II, 1-10, for example, despite their sexual references, but he cuts "e veduta la malvagità de' cherici" from the headnote to I 2, substitutes "Scolare" and "Maestro" for "monaco" and "abate" in I 4 and omits all of I 6, which has nothing to do with sex but much with "la malvagia ipocresia de' religiosi." The headnotes to III reflect the same special interests: the monk becomes a scholar (4), the abbot a necromancer (8) and Masetto (1) is returned from his nunnery to the *"giardino di damigelle"* where Boccaccio found him in the *Novellino*.

It is doubtful that Borghini and his fellow members of the Florentine Academy enjoyed "this forced mutilation of one of Florence's most revered authors," for they apparently "did their best to reduce to a minimum the proportions of the inevitable damage."[8] Religious hypocrisy, for example, although no longer countenanced among ecclesiastical characters, was still allowed the laity: Tedaldo (III 7) yet appears "in forma di peregrino"; the lustful lady of III 3, "sotto spetie di confessione, et di purissima coscienza," deceives a friar who is admittedly "tondo, & grosso . . . nondimeno . . . di santissima vita"; Ricciardo's fraudulent fast-days are still detailed and his "mal foro" clarified in a three-page annotation similar to Ruscelli's (sigs. iiv[r] kiv[r], G3[v]-G4[v]).

But some of Boccaccio's wittiest points were bound to be blunted by the characters' changes in vocations and settings: the closing comment of III 1 about Masetto's adorning Christ's crown with horns makes no sense without the nuns; there is less of a religious mood (and therefore less comic potential) in Puccio's being taught "come egli diverrà beato" by a scholar (III 4), a fact underscored by the weakening of Isabetta's last lines to her lover from "Tu fai fare la penitenzia a *frate* Puccio, per la quale noi abbiamo guadagnato il *paradiso*" to "Tu fai fare la penitenzia a Puccio, per la quale noi habbiamo guadagnato grandissima consolatione" (sig. kviii^v; italics added). Borghini is most scrupulous about blasphemy and treats even nonexistent saints with utmost respect. It is understandable why "fortuna" must replace "san Giuliano" as Rinaldo's guide to the widow's hospitality (II 2; sig. div^v), but it is downright fastidious to remove the "santo Cresci" with which Marato comforts Alatiel (II 7; sig. fviii^v). Isabetta is of course still allowed to ride "senza sella," though not upon "la bestia di san Benedetto o vero di san Giovanni Gualberto" (III 4; sigs. kviii^r-kviii^v).

Given such insensitivity, we can see why blasphemy as respectable as Neifile's illustrations of God's will in III 9 should pass unchallenged while Rustico and his devil are exorcised from III 10. What Boccaccio intended as a final comment on sexually motivated religious hypocrisy is here, from Dioneo's opening thesis, reduced to a series of asterisked expurgations: "Gratiose Donne voi non udiste forse mai dire, * & percio senza partirmi guari dallo effetto . . ." (sig. niii^r). It is tempting to suppose that the Florentine academicians at least partly grasped the Third Day's "effetto" and that every asterisk signified their protests against subverting it. On the other hand, if Borghini did not understand the full significance of his omissions, he was nevertheless conscientious enough to mark them off.

Borghini's revisions, of course, struck his fellow Florentines as excessive and the Roman Curia as inadequate. Between those who had begun to censure the *Decameron* on moral as well as religious grounds and those whose consuming desire was to promote the interests of the national tongue and its finest prose model,[9] there was little room for compromise. Within two years of Borghini's death (1580), one of his Florentine assistants, Lionardo Salviati, cast another vote for Rome against Tuscany with a second revision, a "totally new book such as neither the 1573 correctors nor the Inquisition of that time, and least of all Boccaccio, had ever remotely visualized," a *"Decameron* uncompromisingly remodelled to conform to the exigencies of the extremist moralistic critical current of the times."[10] Its first readers needed only to glance at the italics and asterisks of the prefatory *Tavola* to sense how Salviati had outdone his predecessor. While "un *giovane"* and "suo *superiore"* approximate Borghini's "Scolare" and "Maestro" in the headnote to I 4, the *Decameron's* opening story, untouched by Borghini, now loses its main point: "Ser Ciappelletto con una falsa confessione inganna un santo frate, e muorsi *." Cepparello's death, originally intended as a satiric point of departure ("ed . . .è morto reputato per santo e chiamato san Ciappelletto"), has now become the concluding moral. An even greater boldness is revealed in Salviati's restoring—or should we say mutilating and returning?—the one tale wholly expurgated in 1573 (I 6), though its protagonist now confounds "la malvagia *avarizia* de' *giudici."*

As we might expect, the religious-sexual interplay of the Third Day offered the greatest challenge to Salviati's ingenuity. With Borghini's lead, he neutralizes some insults to the Church by secularizing the characters' vocations and settings. Masetto (III 1), for example, is exiled even farther from his original nunnery to a *"serraglio* di donne,"* all of whom betray the chastity "promessa al Soldano [di Babilonia] ." Similarly, III 3's friar, whom Borghini allowed to be tricked through a lustful lady's sanctimonious confession, is replaced by a "solenne *pedagogo"* drawn into a *"Querimonia,"* while Boccaccio's abbot (III 8), following Borghini's necromancer, turns into an even less offensive doctor of medicine who lived under Tiberius Nero. And even where the clergy had never been involved (III 5) or had been replaced by the laity (III 4), Salviati remained more sensitive to moral issues. Il Zima is allowed to win Francesco's daughter , not his wife; while striving to become *"ricchissimo,"* not "beato," Puccio also loses his daughter, a loss that inspires the editor's marginal caveat against "L'avarizia." Perhaps Salviati's cleverest manipulation of text to complement moral gloss is found in II 7. Both Boccaccio and Borghini have chaste Alatiel shipwrecked and treacherously seduced "tra cristiani." By putting her "tra *li turchi,"* Salviati not only avoids some less than honorable Christian behavior but also removes a barrier to moralizing Alatiel's awakened sexual desires: "Ricordisi il lettore, che questa donna era barbara, e di legge infedele" (sig. f6ᵛ).

For all his careful changes within the text and copious glosses without, Salviati decided that some tales required nothing less than radically revised plots. It was not enough to make Ermellina the daughter rather than the wife of Aldobrandino (III 7) while the margin identified Tedaldo as a counterfeit pilgrim (sig. 17ᵛ); Boccaccio notwithstanding, his editor assures us that the lovers had long been secretly married. Similarly, the several marginal warnings against jealousy in III 6 are rigorously enforced by Salviati's new ending: Catella only *"fece sembiante di rappacificarsi"* with Ricciardo; haunted by memories of her "sciocchezza," she dies of "malinconia" while her seducer, "dolente del suo peccato, in un diserto, faccendo penitenza, finì la vita sua" (sig. 15ʳ). For III 10, on the other hand, the best solution was to preserve the beginning and end ("Alibech va nel diserto * poi quindi tolta, moglie divien di Neerbale"), mutilate the middle (one page alone features seventy-six asterisks!) and make excuses in the margin: "Si lasciano questi fragmenti per salvare piu parole, e piu modi di favellare, che si puo" (sig. n3ʳ). Most important, however, is that the sensitive Salviati betrays some anxiety even with the relatively innocent *All's Well* story. When Giletta observes that she and the widow are "delle nimiche della fortuna," the margin immediately depersonalizes that goddess: "Cioè degli acidenti, ch[e] porta seco i[l] viverci" (sig. nlʳ).

By far the most earnest of Boccaccio's editors and translators is the anonymous author of the 1620 *Decameron* in English, very likely John Florio, who drew upon Salviati's moral refinements and le Maçon's subtlety of expression to produce a version uniquely solemn and decorous.[11] Lacking Painter's freedom to condemn five-sixths of the *Decameron* to "perpetual prison," Florio reads into the whole work a purpose quite alien to its generally carefree spirit. Though many of Boccaccio's "singular and exquisite Histories" have "(long since) bene published before," Florio insists in the epistle dedicatory, they have lacked his "singular morall applications. For, as it was his full scope and ayme, by discovering all vices in their ugly deformities, to make their mortall enemies (the sacred Vertues) to shine the clearer, . . . so every true and upright judgement, in observing the course of these well-carried Novels, shall plainely perceive, that there is not spare made of reproofe in any degree whatsoever, where sin is embraced, and grace neglected. . . . In imitation of witty Aesope, who reciteth not a Fable, but graceth it with a judicious morall application."[12]

Having announced his thesis, the determined moralist at once proceeds to revise all evidence accordingly. Those sexual details of I 4 which Borghini allowed and Salviati amended only slightly are now wholly suppressed or stigmatized (e.g., "Upon this immodest meditation," fol. D6ʳ), and the widow's "concupiscevole appetito" (II 2), which escaped even Salviati's asterisks, yields to a hurried yet proper "wedding and bedding . . . both effected before the bright morning" (fol. G3ᵛ). Ironically enough, though, while Florio's Protestant piety sometimes takes him farther from Boccaccio's plots than Salviati's Catholic zeal, that same piety—or prejudice—often brings him closer to the *Decameron*'s satiric intentions. The leading characters of I 4 are once again monk and abbot, and Saint Julian is recalled to guide Rinaldo to the widow's hospitality. Similarly, the simony and sodomy of the Roman clergy, which Florio again found in his unexpurgated le Maçon (I 2), are emphasized to support his view of Boccaccio as a religious reformer.

But Florio's desire to reveal Boccaccio's anti-Catholic attitudes is not so strong as his respect for Christian decency. While rejecting Salviati's screening of friar and confessional with *"pedagogo"* and *"Querimonia"* in III 3—indeed, Florio had every reason to emphasize the evil that could lurk "Under colour of Confession"—he is also conscious of the friar's devoutness and moralizes the tale accordingly: "Declaring, that the leude and naughty qualities of some persons, doe oftentimes misguide good people, into very great and greevous errors" (fol. Q1ʳ). And since true piety, no matter how misguided, is never to be mocked, Florio accepts Salviati's secularizing of III 4, only adding that Puccio died "before the date of his limitted time, because hee failed of the Philosophers Stone" (fol. Q6ʳ). It must have been a like respect for "morality," not the Curia, that kept Alatiel among Salviati's Turks and omitted Marato's "santo Cresci" (II 7), returned the abbot and his fraudulent purgatory to III 8 while rejecting Boccaccio's observation (via le Maçon) that the adulterous affair continued after Ferondo's deliverance.

Between the contrary directions of le Maçon's text, Rouillé's prefatory morals, and Salviati's moral refinements, Florio was of course occasionally bound to stumble. Following the French Boccaccio, Florio returns Masetto (III 1) to "a Monastery of Nunnes" in the headnote (fol. P1ᵛ), next borrows Rouillé's specious moral "that Virginity is very hardly to be kept, in all places," and then turns to Salviati for the nunnery's locale ("Not farre from *Alexandria*" there were "divers virgins . . . vowed to . . . the Soldan of *Babylon*"). But once these pagan ladies evince their frailty, the context, inspired by le Maçon, turns Catholic— "*Ave Maria* Sister (said the other Nunne) what kinde of words are these you utter? Doe not you know, that wee have promised our virginity to God?"—while the margin becomes Protestant: "Example, at least excuses formed to that intent, prevaileth much with such kind of religious women."[13] Similar discrepancies are found in III 6, where Florio uses Rouillé's moral ("Declaring, how much perseverance, and a couragious spirit is availeable in love") to introduce not the joyously sensual original but Salviati's revision, which has both lovers dying of remorse.

While Florio's care in deleting or inserting allusions to other tales may reveal a "keen . . . sense of [narrative] cohesion,"[14] his obsession with moral applications surely dulled his sense of Boccaccio's thematic interplay. We cannot know whether Florio ever questioned the applicability of prefatory morals to stories in le Maçon, or wondered why those morals were missing in Salviati, or became uneasy as he realized that Salviati's characters and settings were merely secularized versions of le Maçon's. As he approached the *All's Well* story, however, he must have noticed, even more than Painter befor him, that the Third Day's stories were especially troublesome for any moralist. Painter, after all, had no italicized and asterisked Salviati to point up the difficulties, only the unruffled Ruscelli. Despite such evidence that Boccaccio was linking sexually motivated, *religious* rationalizings, though, Florio apparently thought only of morality as he alternated between le Maçon's religious and Salviati's secular contexts.

Most of Florio's treatment of III 9 is therefore predictable. He first cites the moral Rouillé probably found in Giolito: "Commending the good judgement and understanding in Ladies or Gentlewomen, that are of a quicke and apprehensive spirit" (fol. T5ᵛ). He faithfully translates the inital dramatic interplay, including Neifile's concern that

after Lauretta's "rare and wittie discourse," the narrators "yet remaining, are the more to be feared and suspected." Aside from adding
that the virtuous maid pursued by Bertrand "was worthily married, to
her Mothers great comfort" (fol. U3ʳ), Florio follows his two now
congruent texts quite closely, here adding a rhetorical flourish—e.g.,
"*Bertrand* . . . being the onely Saint that caused her pilgrimage" (fol.
T6ʳ)—there emphasizing the "honest office" of the widow in the
bed-plot (fol. U3ʳ). Nor does the essentially humorless translator
convey Boccaccio's mischievous mood in his explanation that "the
King saw her . . . [as] a faire, comely, and discreete young Gentle-
woman; wherefore, hee would no longer hide it [the fistula "on his
stomacke"], but layed it open to her view" (fol. T6ʳ).

But if Salviati was concerned about Giletta's careless tribute to the
power "della fortuna," Florio reveals an even greater sense of uneasiness over her frequent appeals to God's will. During Giletta's first
confrontation with France, Boccaccio (and after him, Salviati) has her
invoke the name of "Dio" or "Iddio" three times. While le Maçon
accurately renders both terms as "Dieu" (sig. P6ᵛ), the more cautious
Florio substitutes "heaven" in all three instances. Similarly, whereas
Boccaccio's and Salviati's heroine arranges the bed-trick hoping that
"mi farà Iddio grazia d'ingravidare" (sig. N1ᵛ) and le Maçon's trusts
"que nostre Seigneur me fera tant de grace de devenir grosse" (sig.
P8ᵛ), Florio's simply puts her faith in "faire Fortune" (fol. U2ᵛ).
Do these changes reflect a calculated attempt to avoid the blasphemy
that escaped even the sensitive Salviati? What else explains Florio's
turning "come fu piacer di Dio, la donna ingravidò" (sig. N1ᵛ) and/or
"nostre Seigneur voulut que la Comtesse devint grosse" (sig. Q1ʳ)
into "the houre proving so auspicious, and *Juno* being Lady of the
ascendent, conjoyned with the witty *Mercury,* shee conceived" (fol.
U3ʳ)? Here, apparently, the wheel has come full circle. Florio's earnest
desire to prove Boccaccio moral destroys Neifile's equally earnest
desire to prove Giletta virtuous. Lost in the confrontation is not only
God's seal of approval but Boccaccio's high comedy.

Having thus mutilated the Third Day's theme of shaping divinity,
Florio proceeds to his most brazen bowdlerizing, completely under-
mining the interplay Boccaccio employs to emphasize Neifile's naivete.
Since le Maçon offered a version of III 10 no less racy than the original,

and Salviati only a mass of italics and asterisks, Florio was obliged to start anew. "Gracious Ladies," observes a no longer roguish Dioneo, "I know that you do now expect from me, some such queint Tale, as shall be suteable to my merry disposition, rather savouring of wantonnesse, then any discreet and sober wisedom, and such a purpose indeed, I once had entertained" (fol. Ut^r). Dioneo, however, has been strangely converted by his fellows' stories, and so strongly does he protest his reformation that we may suspect that Florio noticed the very undercutting he was in the process of concealing: "But having well observed all your severall relations, grounded on grave and worthy examples, especially the last, so notably delivered by the Queene, I cannot but commend faire *Juliet* of *Narbona,* in perfourming two such strange impossibilities, and conquering the unkindnesse of so cruel a husband. If my Tale come short of the precedent excellency, . . . accept my good will, and let me stand engaged for a better heereafter."

Appropriating "The Annales of *Denmarke*" (or, more accurately, the seventy-fifth tale of Belleforest's *Histoires tragiques*[15]), the reformed Dioneo celebrates no devil in hell but "The wonderfull and chaste resolved continency of faire Serictha, daughter to Siwalde King of Denmarke, who being sought and sued unto by many worthy persons, that did affect her dearly, would not looke any man in the face, untill such time as she was married" (fol. U4^r)—even, we might add, while she was about to be ravished (see fol. Aa2^r). Instead of providing Boccaccio's counterpoint, Dioneo now piously shoulders the burden of Belleforest's rhetoric and Florio's moral applications. And though his ferociously chaste story is allegedly "commended by all the company, and so much the rather, because it was free from all folly and obscoennesse" (fol. Aa6^r), this is but a small reward for sacrificing his important role in Boccaccio's now-ruined design. Borghini's and Salviati's treatments of Dioneo had been kinder; being silenced is preferable to being distorted. With far less respect for his text than his predecessors, never indicating what he is altering or omitting, Florio takes us even farther from Boccaccio. Surely nothing could be more contradictory to the Third Day's spirit than his last complacent picture of "*Dioneus,* being out of his wonted wanton element" (fol. Aa6^v).

The spirit in which Shakespeare took the Third Day's storytelling can of course only be inferred from his own version, especially as that version, in its handling of traditional elements, touches on the story's traditional meanings. But since the meanings that accrued in the editions published between Delfino's (1516) and Florio's (1620) are so varied, we might profitably preface our examination of *All's Well* with a brief survey of the treatments of III 9 most likely to have influenced the play's shaping. Primarily owing to its linguistic accessibility, almost every scholar has listed Painter's translation as Shakespeare's sole source. From Painter alone the playwright would have received a relatively accurate version of III 9, but completely divorced from the Third Day's dramatic and thematic interplay. Without the very means Boccaccio employs to enrich the significance of the Queen's story, Shakespeare could not have inferred any meaning other than the one Neifile intended, though he might have wondered why Painter was uneasy about five-sixths of the *Decameron* and had passed over Giletta in his prefatory moralizings. While Painter's immense popularity makes it likely that Shakespeare began with his version, his habit of remarking upon (and thereby stimulating interest in) the great writers he has anthologized makes it almost as likely that Shakespeare did not end with him. Surely the playwright who invariably consulted several chronicles for each history play and almost always more than one novella for every comedy and tragedy would have been prone to look farther than Painter.

Assuming that Shakespeare was intrigued by but not fully content with Painter's rendition, what other versions were readily available? None in English, evidently, despite the claim of Boccaccio's friend, Franco Sacchetti, that the *Decameron* had been "in Inghilterra . . . ridotto alla loro lingua."[16] Willard Farnham long ago argued that except for a few isolated, Latinized tales, the *Decameron* was virtually unknown to England until well into the sixteenth century, and the later detailed study of Herbert B. Wright appears to bear this out.[17] So do the seven-hundred-odd pages of Elizabethan criticism edited by G. Gregory Smith, which never allude to the *Decameron* and only four times to Boccaccio's poetry.[18]

About the same time that Painter was popularizing Boccaccio, however, Ascham was reminiscing over Lady Jane Grey reading Plato "in Greeke . . . with as moch delite, as som jentleman wold read a merie tale in *Bocase*" and condemning those who attend "our Godlie Italian

Chirch" in London only "to heare the Italian tonge naturally spoken, not to heare Gods doctrine trewly preached."[19] Supplementing such indirect instruction were the lessons offered in person and in print by men like Hollyband and Florio. However they came by their facility, Turberville, Whetstone, and several lesser Elizabethan storytellers seem to have borrowed directly from the *Decameron* in Italian, whereas littcrateurs like "H. C." and Robert Greene reveal their dependence on le Maçon.[20] And contrary to Dr. Johnson's opinion that Shakespeare knew no modern language but his own—he "read little more than English and chose for his fables only such tales as he found translated"—most scholars today "allow Shakespeare some French and Italian."[21] To conclude otherwise, we must account for the numerous authors Shakespeare shows a detailed knowledge of who remained untranslated in his own time: Ser Giovanni Fiorentino, Bandello, Cinthio, Masuccio, Boisteau, and Belleforest, to name only the least debatable.

Granting Shakespeare the not uncommon ability to read Italian does not of course insure his awareness of the Third Day's ironic interplay; whereas Boccaccio's design is easily inferable in the editions of Ruscelli and Giolito, it is obscured by the moral-ecclesiastical expurgating of Borghini and Salviati. But the most probable guide to the *Decameron*'s real spirit was the man who had helped Painter through Ruscelli, le Maçon. As Professor Wright has observed, about the time Shakespeare was lodging with the Huguenot Montjoy family (c. 1604), he worked into several plays French names, terms, phrases, and dialogue, and *All's Well* is no exception: Parolles, who "love[s] not many words"; Lavatch, who has "not much skill in grass"; "young Charbon the puritan and old Poysam the papist" (cf. *chair bonne, poisson*); an instance of "cardecue" (for "quart d'écu") earlier than that recorded as first by the *OED*; Helena's feigned pilgrimage to "Saint Jaques le Grand."[22] To such indications of Shakespeare's interest and ability in French, Wright adds a list of characters and places in *All's Well* whose spellings come closer to le Maçon's than to Painter's. Bertram, for example, is more like the French "Bertrand" than Painter's "Beltramo." Similarly, whereas Painter always reads "Gerardo of Narbona," Shakespeare has "Gerard de Narbon," probably an approximation of "Gerard de Narbonne." Although Painter's own partial dependence on le Maçon sometimes obscures these relationships, Wright concludes that Shakespeare's "Senoys," "Rossillion," and "Violenta" are also better accounted for by the French intermediary than the English.[23]

By allowing Shakespeare any of the eighteen sixteenth-century editions of le Maçon, we establish as a potential source one of the richest, most accurate, and sensitive treatments of the *Decameron.* It is quite possible that the playwright went on to read one or more of the Italian editions we have examined: Ruscelli's, which Painter advertises; the earlier but often published and heavily glossed tome by Giolito; Borghini's single, highly influential issue; Salviati's even more influential (and even more misleading) version. Since we seek not only full-blown models but sources of information, we cannot afford to overlook the smallest springboard for Shakespeare's imagination— a marginal comment, an italicized phrase, even an asterisk. The same cautious sense of perspective we tried to use in dealing with the frequently printed *Virginia* and the relatively obscure *Le Chevalereux Comte d'Artois* must also obtain here. As we attempt to establish certainties, we must be patient with probabilities. The Elizabethans never refer to the French romance; there seems to have been no way for them to have known it.[24] Those who knew Castiglione, on the other hand, knew of Accolti, though only Harvey speaks of his comedy.[25]

Even Florio, who came too late to help Shakespeare write *All's Well,* offers us some help in reading it. At least partly aware of Dioneo's original function and clearly embarrassed by Neifile's claims concerning God's role in Giletta's success, Florio feels morally safer upon secular ground and therefore continually minimizes his texts' religious frames of reference. It is perhaps fitting that this last contributor to the *All's Well* story should show how little inclined the tradition was to celebrate the heroine's spiritual qualities. Neifile's attempt is parodied by Dioneo. Virginia's piety turns to a "pietoso inganno." Those who translate or edit the *Decameron,* on the other hand, generally admire Giletta, but only for her ingenuity: Painter refuses to moralize her story; Salviati and Florio are uneasy about her allusions to Fortune and God. Only the Countess of Artois walks hand in hand with the Blessed Virgin, and she is obviously an anomaly.

Granted, Shakespeare was just as free to make Helena unambiguously sympathetic, free even to validate her spiritual credentials and to turn the story into the parable of redemption that critics like G. Wilson Knight have found it. But Shakespeare was not free to be misunderstood. Whichever new direction he wished to take his audience, he would have to begin with and make allowances for their expectations. And do not the treatments of III 9 surrounding Shakespeare's imply that his audience anticipated wit, irony, and skepticism rather than fairy-tale motifs or Virtue-Story conventions? In our concluding chapter we shall see how Shakespeare honored those expectations by inventing characters and incidents that exploit that tradition's darker meanings. Before turning to the play as a whole, however, it may be helpful to deal with a few of its most troublesome scenes, events that seem more realistic-topical than literary-traditional, all ultimately drawn from Shakespeare's library but each clearly appealing to his England for its measure if significance. It is when Shakespeare brings the old story closest to home that we are most likely to detect his understanding of it.

NOTES

1. See Edward Hutton's introduction to *The Decameron,* ed. W. E. Henley, I, cxix.

2. These editions are listed by Herbert G. Wright, *The First English Translation of the 'Decameron,'* p. 266.

3. *Le Decameron de M. Jehan Bocace Florentin* (Paris, 1559), sig. Al^v. All citations to le Macon are to this edition.

4. See Wright, *First English,* pp. 9, 188, 266-67.

5. Ed. Joseph Jacobs, I, 5. All citations to Painter are to the three-volume Dover rpt. of the 1890 Jacobs's ed.

6. I, 5, 11. In the first tome Painter permits ten tales (translations of I, 3, 8, 10; II, 2, 3, 4, 5, 8; III, 9; IV, 1); in the second tome he includes another six (I, 5; VIII, 7; X, 3, 4, 5, 9), and he concludes by listing eight authors (not including Boccaccio) whose works he has not yet exhausted. It is quite possible that a careful counting prefaced Painter's reference to "the sixt part."

7. See Herbert G. Wright, "The Indebtedness of Painter's Translations from Boccaccio in 'The Palace of Pleasure' to the French Version of le Macon," pp. 431-35.

8. Peter M. Brown, *Lionardo Salviati: A Critical Biography,* p. 162.

9. Ibid., pp. 163-65.

10. Ibid., p. 167. All citations to Salviati are to the third (Venice, 1585) edition.

11. See Wright, *First English*, pp. 30, 34.

12. *The Decameron Containing An hundred pleasant Novels* (London, 1620), fol. A2ᵛ. All citations to Florio are to this edition.

13. Fols. P3ʳ-P3ᵛ. Wright, *First English*, notes that this is Florio's only subjective marginal comment and that the nun's oath comes from le Macon's "Oime" (pp. 44, 179).

14. Ibid., p. 70.

15. Ibid., p. 52.

16. *Proemio del trecento novelle* (c. 1399), as cited by Mary Augusta Scott, *Elizabethan Translations from the Italian*, p. 92.

17. See Farnham, "England's Discovery of the *Decameron*," pp. 123-39, and Wright, *Boccaccio in England from Chaucer to Tennyson*, pp. 111-88.

18. See *Elizabethan Critical Essays*, I, 132, 152; II, 319, 369.

19. *The Schoolmaster*, ed. John E. B. Mayor, pp. 96-97, 138.

20. See Wright, *Boccaccio in England*, pp. 142-70.

21. Geoffrey Bullough, *Narrative and Dramatic Sources of Shakespeare*, I, x.

22. Herbert G. Wright, "How Did Shakespeare Come to Know the 'Decameron'?," pp. 45-46.

23. Ibid., pp. 46-48.

24. See p. 71, n. 39.

25. See Smith, *Essays*, I, 125.

VI
From Westminster to Santiago:
All's Well's Nonliterary Contexts

> We come lastly to the matter of wards and such other burdens
> (for so we acknowledge them) as to the tenures *in capite* and knight-
> service are incident. . . . This prerogative of the crown, which we
> desire to compound for, [has been] matter of mere profit, and
> not of any honour at all or princely dignity. . . . [And] with how
> great grievance and damage of the subject, to the decay of many
> houses and disabling of them to serve their prince and country;
> with how great mischief also, by occasion of many forced and
> ill-suited marriages; and lastly, with how great contempt and
> reproach of our nation in foreign countries, how small a commodity
> now was raised to the crown in respect of that, which with great
> love and joy and thankfulness, for the restitution of this original
> right in disposing of our children, we would be content and glad
> to assure unto your Majesty.
>
> "Apology of the House of Commons," 20 June, 1604

The search for topical meanings in Tudor drama, as David
Bevington reminds us, "has a long history—much of it inglorious."[1]
Swinburne's facetious revelation of Romeo as a subtle shadowing
of Lord Burghley in no way dampened his contemporaries' enthusiasm
for discovering the "real" people represented in plays as promising as
Endymion and *Hamlet,* and in our own time Mario Praz complains
about the "perverse ingenuity" with which G. Lambin identifies "the
names of the captains given by Parolles in *All's Well,* IV, iii, 165 ff.,
with historical supporters of the French League."[2] Less obviously
topical than many Elizabethan and Jacobean plays, *All's Well* has
attracted fewer and usually saner historical glosses, though Bevington,

who is always "skeptical of topical identification of historical personages and particular events," notices some old and new overreadings: a comedy "critical of the Essex camp, for Bertram's dutifulness toward his mother and his reluctance to marry call back memories of Southampton and Elizabeth Vernon"; Parolles as "Pearse Edmonds, a minion of Southampton's and hence a rival of Shakespeare, [so that] the motivation for Shakespeare's soured disposition becomes clear."[3]

As a rule, any examination of *All's Well*'s nonliterary contexts should recall Bevington's well supported contention that topical meaning is better studied in terms of general issues than particular personalities. It is helpful, for example, to set next to Lavatch's "Service is no heritage"[4] not only the proverbs listed by M. P. Tilley[5] but also a pamphlet noted by G. B. Harrison,[6] *A Health to the Gentlemanly Profession of Serving-men* (1598). Not that this seventy-two page complaint against the servant's rapidly diminishing lot reveals a personality or unlocks a theme. But as an indictment against the niggardliness of masters and the sad situations of masterless men, the pamphlet confirms our impression that *All's Well* is taking us even farther from fairy-tale problems than any of its sources or analogues. More pointed yet less helpful, on the other hand, is Robert G. Hunter's conjecture that the heroine's name was intended to suggest not only Helen of Troy but Saint Helena, mother of Constantine the Great and discoverer of the True Cross, "by means of which she healed the sick and raised the dead."[7] As evidence that this British saint "was by no means forgotten by Shakespeare's contemporaries," Hunter cites only Holinshed, who, he admits, "is very cautious about [her] historicity" and, we might add, even less assured concerning the Cross ("Some writers alledge") and her miracles ("as it is reported, but how truelie I cannot tell").[8] Given Holinshed's skepticism and Hunter's own admission that "Protestant historians tended to take a jaundiced view of her story," it is difficult to follow his conclusion that "her name would presumably have had sacred connotations for the average Londoner."[9] Equally important, whereas the play often alludes to and exploits its affinities with *Troilius and Cressida,* it shares nothing specific with the Legend of Saint Helena.

Perhaps the most intricate argument for dating *All's Well* was made by the editors of the "New Shakespeare" on the basis of several allegedly topical references: (1) Helena's "Bless our poor virginity from under-miners and blowers-up" (I. i. 120-21) and the Second Lord's warning about traitors who "attain to their abhorr'd ends" (IV. iii. 23) allude to the Gunpowder Plot of November 5, 1605; (2) Lavatch's "surplice of humility over the black gown of a big heart" (I. iii. 94-95) recognizes Bancroft's enforcement of the surplice upon the puritan clergy in 1604-05; (3) Bertram's resentment at being "kept a coil with" and "the forehorse to a smock" (II. i. 27 ff.) and his consequent decision to "steal away" before all "honor be bought up" reflects so closely the situation of Elizabeth's young favorites that it could "scarcely have been written after 1603."[10] Against such evidence that the play was written for Elizabethans and revised for Jacobeans, G. K. Hunter argues that the allusions to the Gunpowder Plot are insubstantial, that the vestment controversy had been flaring up and down for more than fifty years, and that while Bertram's situation in II. i. is essentially that of Elizabeth's young courtiers, it would not be pointless for an audience of the next reign—"Shakespeare . . . depicts the unknown by means of the known, but the known need not be contemporary."[11] From these three topical allusions, then, we gain only two certainties: (1) the play touches on at least one religious controversy that had run throughout Elizabeth's reign and (2) the play sometimes shapes Bertram along the lines of Elizabeth's favorites. The unlikely choice of Mars's novice as "general of our horse" (III. iii. 1), for example, seems less strange, though no less capricious, when we recall that both Essex and Southampton were at different times Master of the Horse.

If *All's Well*'s topical references fail to pinpoint its period of composi-tion, they are even less helpful in determining the time it represents. Which French monarch are we supposed to see in the King who bids his young lords to "Let higher Italy / (Those bated that inherit but the fall / Of the last monarchy) see that you come / Not to woo honor, but to wed it" (II. i. 12-15)? The ambiguous "higher" (socially or geo-graphically?) and "bated" ("depressed" or "excepted"?) make it even harder to identify "the last monarchy." The "New Shakespeare" rejects both "the Roman Empire" and "the reign of the emperor Charles V," for "Surely the reference is to the decline of the great house of the Medici, after the death of Cosimo, . . . in 1574, a period . . . when Florence was permeated by . . . corruption.[12] But G. K. Hunter sees "a direct reference to the doctrine of the four monarchies or empires, derived from Daniel, ii. 31 ff and common in Christian historiography," the last representing the Holy Roman Empire or the Papal monarchy,[13] depending on one's religious persuasion. The most direct identification of the King, though, is made by a surgeon Shakespearean, Alban H. G. Doran, who naturally examines the medical evidence: "probably Charles V of France, who suffered from a thoracic fistula."[14]

Granting Shakespeare's frequent anachronisms, there is no reason why the King could not have had several centuries of fallen monarchs as his contemporaries. The identification that seems the most far-fetched, however, may shed the greatest light. Medieval and Renaissance Italy offered Shakespeare dozens of last monarchies, but only one French king answered to Boccaccio's portrait of a desperately ill sovereign, Charles the Wise (1364-80), who reigned a little too late for the *Decameron* but not too early to attract Shakespeare's notice. Assuming that Shakespeare had already consulted Lord Berner's translation of Froissart's *Chronicles* for *Richard II,* he could not have completely forgotten Froissart's intervening accounts of the "right sage and subtell"[15] king whose reign overlapped Richard's. And in the historian's epitaph for the man who spent his whole life fending off his enemies and infirmities with patience and cunning, Shakespeare encountered something more like fairy tale than any episode in Boccaccio's fiction:

It was of trouthe . . . that the kynge of Naverr, whan the frenche kyng was but duke of Normandy, . . . wolde have poysoned him; so that the kyng receyved the poison, and . . . all the heare of his body went of, and all the nayles of his handes and fete, and than all his body became as drie as a staffe, so that he was without remedy. The emperoure of Rome his uncle, whan he herde speakynge of his malady, he sent hym a conyng phicycion, the greattest mayster reputed in that arte that was as than in all the worlde. Whan this mayster was come . . . he dyde there one of the greattest cures that hath been herde of, for he kylled the venym within hym, or the best parte therof, . . . and made hym hole. . . . This venym ever yssued out of hym lytell and lytell at [under?] his arme by a lytell pype [cf. Latin *fistula*] ; and whan this mayster departed out of Fraunce, he gave the kynge a receyte to use as

long as he lyved, and he sayd, . . . Loke whan this yssue by this
pype drieth up, than surely ye shall dye; but ye shall have a fyftene
dayes respyte after ye fall sicke or ever ye dye, to remember your
soule. So the kynge remembred well his wordes, and bare this
pype xxii. days [years?], which thynge often tymes abasshed
hym.[16]

If Shakespeare, while seeking material with which to flesh out
Boccaccio's brief narrative, recollected this strange passage, he could
have returned to Froissart for two elements which appear only in his
version of the *All's Well* story. First, the political atmosphere engen-
dered as nations "by th' ears" both receive help from a deciding
foreign power, "One of the greatest in the Christian world" (I. ii. 1;
IV. iv. 2). What Clifford Leech regards as evidence of a world "where
high politics [are] murky"[17] is even more obvious in Froissart's
account of Charles V's political opportunism during the Hundred
Years' War. "No man ever knew so well how to dissemble" is merely
modern shorthand for the medieval chronicler's lengthy accounts of
how "the frenche king all this season secretly and subtelly" managed
this or that.[18] Secondly, Froissart offered Shakespeare a royal confidant as well as a king, Charles's strong right arm, the fearless Breton,
Sir Bertrand Du Guesclin. Granting all the differences between this
fiery fellow and old Lafew (*le feu?*), each is by far his liege's foremost
courtier. Charles created the poor gentleman of Brittany Constable of
France, the realm's highest rank, and the modern view that he had
"little love for any one excpet Du Guesclin" again finds its basis in
Froissart's report that Charles, only two months before his own death,
had his friend's body "caryed to saynt Denyse, . . . and there he was
layde in sepulture, nere to the tombe of kynge Charles, which the
kynge had made for hym[self] in his dayes: and so he laye at the
kynges fete; and there his obsequy was done right honorably, as though
he hadde ben the kynges sonne."[19]

Although we cannot afford to overlook such potential sources of
inspiration, we must distinguish between material that may have
influenced Shakespeare and material that Shakespeare clearly used to
influence his audience, the difference, for example, between our obscure
(perhaps chance) analogue in Froissart and allusions that seem calculated

to raise up memories of Essex (or rather, Essexian situations). Only those nonliterary contexts which Shakespeare invokes will illuminate the play, and they are usually of a general nature, drawn from and appealing to four facets of Elizabethan life: the law, medicine, politics, and religion.

The contemporary legal world is manifested by *All's Well's* highlighting of wardship and enforced marriage, prerogatives whose odiousness by the turn of the century is but barely hinted at in the epigraph to this chapter. The system Parliament found dishonorable, damaging and contemptible about the same time as the play's first performance was, according to Sir John Neale, "a breeding-ground of corruption,"[20] within which, adds H. E. Bell, "the sale of marriages . . . constituted the most spectacular evil."[21] But the most detailed modern indictment of wardship is made by Joel Hurstfield, who concentrates on its personal and social consequences and underlines its anachronisms.[22] The tenures Parliament would compound with the Crown for hearken back to Norman—perhaps even pre-Norman—military feudalism or "tenure by knight-service," a system in which kings and barons, as tenants-in-chief, granted land to their inferiors in exchange for military service. Whenever the holder, great or small, died leaving as heir a child too young to render service, the overlord was obliged temporarily to grant the land to someone able to perform that service. The land (and with it the child) were said to have passed into wardship, and the lord, in order to ensure that future service would be efficient and loyal, assumed the right to control his ward's upbringing and, in the case of a female ward, the right of consent to her choice of a husband.

What began as a reasonable arrangement to protect legitimate interests, however, soon developed into what the Jacobean petitioners term "mere profit." By 1250 the lord's logical right of consent to a female ward's marriage had become the power to choose a partner for an heir of either sex; and since what the lords possessed they were free to sell, wardships were turned from military safeguards into articles of trade. The first merchant of the realm was of course the king, for if but one acre of the estate were held of the crown by knight-service in chief, the baron who owned a far larger portion was obliged to yield to "prerogative wardship." And it was for these feudal-financial prospects, Hurstfield argues, that Henry VIII enlarged the Office of Wards into the Court of Wards in 1540. Henry had been selling monastic lands since 1535 and usually at prices lower than market value, but in almost every case "the recipient was required to hold his lands by knight-service of the crown" which "meant little or nothing new except wardship and marriage."[23]

By now it should be clear that Bertram's opening remark about being "now in ward, evermore in subjection" would have suggested nothing good to Shakepseare's audience. Until well into the reign of Charles II, the plight of the ward remained substantially the same. He was usually a royal ward only in name, for his guardianship would soon be sold, usually to a complete stranger. So would "the right to offer him a bride whom he could rarely afford to refuse, for his refusal meant that he must pay a crushing fine to his guardian. Meanwhile his land would also have passed into wardship, either to his guardian or to someone else, for them to snatch a quick profit until the ward was old enough to reclaim his own."[24] Skillful lawyers fabricated bogus transactions to conceal wardships; resourceful bureaucrats paid informers and spies to hunt them down. Wards included children even humbler than Helena, and guardians occasionally proved as humane as the Countess. But from "the shrieve's fool," allegedly "with child" by Captian Dumaine (IV. iii. 187), to the Earl of Southampton, who is reputed to have been fined £5,000 for refusing the granddaughter of his guardian, Lord Burghley, the ward's own welfare seems rarely to have been his protector's main concern.[25]

What response, then, would *All's Well*'s enforced marriage have evoked? Noting how Shakespeare has played up the enforcement motif in Boccaccio, Glenn H. Blayney compares Bertram's situation to that of the unhappy hero of George Wilkins's *The Miseries of Inforst Mariage* (1607): "Perhaps we should today regard Bertram in the light of seventeenth-century attitudes which explained his behavior as a victim of a king's will unjustly imposed through the prerogatives of wardship. Scarborrow, in *The Miseries,* who deserts Katherine as Bertram deserts Helena, was considered, certainly by Wilkins and probably by others, to have been a victim of an unjust guardian's enforcement. Why not Bertram as well?"[26] In several respects the two plays' enforcement scenes are quite similar. Like the King, Scarborrow's guardian, Lord Falconbridge, first moves the marriage with kindness and generosity, praising his ward's character and sincerely believing that marriage will keep him from bad company; though the bride-to-be is the guardian's own niece, Scarborrow's uncle assures us that Falconbridge "speakes like a father for my Kinsman" and that the family's "name is blest in such an honoured marriage."[27] Again like the King, Falconbridge becomes furious at his ward's refusal: "Fell me his wood, make havocke, spoyle and wast," "I'll make you poore inough," "Ile make thee marry to my Chambermaid" (ll. 439, 441, 454).

Falconbridge's last threat, however, touches on a significant difference in the wards' situations which Blayney does not pursue. To justify his hero's disobedience, Wilkins appeals to the relatively modern notion of romantic love as a basis for marriage; moments before Scarborrow rejects a lady *of his own rank,* the audience sees him and the lady of his choice plighting troth. Shakespeare, on the other hand, allows his hero an excuse far less charming but, in Elizabethan eyes at least, probably more valid. For by Elizabeth's time the suing and granting of wardships had become carefully systematized, and no stipualtion was clearer than that "the *maritagium,* the right to marry the ward to whomever the guardian chose," had to be exercised "*absque disparagatione,* without disparagement."[28] Sir Edward Coke, James's lord chief justice, later listed defects of the blood alongside defects of mind and body as disparagements in marriage, and he allowed that any relative of a disparaged ward could "enter and oust the guardian in chivalry" or, failing that, the ward himself could either evict his guardian from the property or bring a lawsuit upon him.[29] When we realize the Falconbridge is no more rigid than many Elizabethan fathers, from Old Capulet to Polixenes, we can see that Wilkins's focus is only incidentally on the miseries of wardship. But if "real" fathers are quite willing to make or break marriages for their children's good, none seeks to disparage his own lineage.[30] Bertram's sarcastic query, "But follows it, my lord, to bring me down / Must answer for your raising?" (ll. iii. 112-13) wittily converys Beltramo's objection ("conoscendo lei non esser di legnaggio che alla sua nobiltà bene stesse"[31]) in as English an idiom as Florio's translation ("yet in regard of her meane birth, which he held as a disparagement to his Nobility in blood"[32]).

At issue in Shakespeare's enforcement scene, therefore, is not whether this handsome youth is a spoiled snob but whether this ward's rights are being violated. The appeal is to legal precedent: the King must answer to "She had her breeding at my father's charge." Bertram may have other, more personal objections to Helena, but he plays his best card first. The difference in rank is definitely not a reason "he concocts," as Margaret Ranald contends, nor is it quite fair to maintain that "The king promptly dismisses that reason by offering to give Helena a title and money."[33] What the king primarily offers is a not-very-prompt, twenty-eight-line dissertation on virtue as the true nobility, a collection of truisms that can be traced from Ascham back to Seneca and Juvenal by way of Chaucer and dozens of his contemporaries. George M. Vogt, who long ago anthologized sixty-eight passages affirming this theme, concluded that "the sentiment is one of those which, gratifying as they do, in a large open-handed fashion, the self-compensatory propensity of the average man (always, necessarily, less powerful than virtuous), lend themselves peculiarly to poetic treatment in all ages and have little to do with the actualities either of the poet's criticism of life or of his practice."[34] Though Vogt's compilation does not pretend to be exhaustive, his conclusion is borne out by the fact that the affirmations are most numerous when class distinctions were least flexible—only four are made after 1700.

While admitting that the Tudor age was a time of some social fluidity, Hurstfield cautions that "this flow of population and wealth could not wash away the rock out of which Tudor society was hewn: degree. Men had no doubt as to their own, and other people's, station in life."[35] In a happy, patently fictional situation Dekker's King might insist that "love respects no blood, / Cares not for difference of birth or state."[36] In a far less romantic setting, Bertram, like Bullingbrook, challenges law, and his King evades the issue with high-minded humanism. But are not such sentiments applied high-handedly? If Vogt's examples are representative, virtue as the true nobility may be used by the lover to excuse his affection but never by an outsider to enforce a choice. Boccaccio, for example, nowhere hints at such egalitarianism in III 9, but he allows Ghismonda, only two stories later, to make an eloquent defense of her love for humble Guiscardo. The King's attempt to waive someone else's rights, in fact, violates the very spirit of the tradition he has invoked. Instead of arguing duty he emphasizes dignity and then rages at independence. Not one of his definitions of "honor" supports his wounded pride—"My honor's at the stake"—or his display of arbitrary power: "It is in us to plant thine honor where / We please to have it grow."

Nor can even this grand guardian dislodge the Tudor rock of degree. Bertram objects to Helena's background, a history that the King cannot rewrite, though he would "create the rest" with "honor and wealth." The same documents that affirm Helen's "nobility dative," the titles she has "derived . . . by direct acquisition from the prince," show that it is a less "desirable kind of nobility" than "nobility native, . . . descent from noble ancestors."[37] For one thing, the child "of the ignoble man, . . . even if he . . . performs worthy deeds, . . . is not actuated by the disinterested love of virtue which inspires the gentleman, but by desire for gain," and "the presumption of superiority in character and ability still lay with the man well-born."[38] Of all Shakespeare's characters, only two achieve native nobility *ex post facto,* Perdita's foster father and brother, each "a gentleman born . . . any time these four hours" (*WT,* V. ii. 135-37). Was there a similar smile behind the King's bestowal of instant nobility upon the daughter of a "poor physician," the "least worthy" of the professions, barely above that of "the barber and the apothecary"?[39] We are told that France has in fact made Helena "the equal in every way of Count Rossillion" and that "in the reigns of Elizabeth and James I, it would have been unwise to deny the monarch's ability to do this."[40] It would have been even less wise for an actor to assume a Scottish accent and speak of "my thirty-pound knights," but it did happen, and only a year or two later.[41]

Motivated not by the King's harangue on honor but by his threats of "revenge and hate / . . . / Without all terms of pity" (11. 164-66), Bertram finally bends:

> Pardon, my *gracious* lord; for I submit
> My fancy to your eyes. When I consider
> What *great* creation and what *dole* of honor
> *Flies* where you bid it, I find that she, which late
> Was in my *nobler* thoughts most *base,* is now
> The praised of the King, who *so ennobled,*
> Is *as 'twere born so.* [11. 167-73; italics added]

But the italicized words suggest that the surrender is not unconditional, that the request for pardon is purely political and tinged with sarcasm, and that had the play ended here, all would still have been unwell. Honors that fly wherever royalty bids underline the theme of authority arbitrarily exercised; we are not surprised to find the play's other ruler, the Duke of Florence, also possessed of "honors that can fly from us" (III. i. 20). Bertram also leaves us questioning where his "nobler thoughts" stand now. There is certainly no hint that the "fancy" he reluctantly submits has actually changed, and in his later refusal to consummate the marriage, the audience porbably saw not only the old disdain but also a renewed hope to escape enforcement through legal means. For without consummation, even the "religiously ratified *de praesenti* matrimonial contract that he has just entered into" is not quite indissoluble; Bertram could later argue, for example, that his consent was obtained "by threats sufficient to arouse fear in a strong man" or "through respect for authority *(per metus reverentialis)*."[42] Finally, the strained logic of the contrained ward—"nobler . . . base . . . so ennobled . . . born so"—implies a satiric tone. Bertram probably intended his argument to sound specious, a capitulation only "as 'twere."

The world of medicine is another facet of Elizabethan life that *All's Well* looks at unromantically. Whether the King's miraculous cure came directly out of Boccaccio's matter-of-fact description or was also influenced by Froissart's mysterious account, Shakespeare surrounds it with topical references: "the schools, / Embowell'd of their doctrine" (I. iii. 240-41); "The congregated college" (II. i. 117); "the artists / . . . both of Galen and Paracelsus" (II. iii. 10-11). Central to C. J. Sisson's article on "Shakespeare's Helena and Dr. William Harvey: With a case-history from Harvey's practice" is that "at all points Helena's intervention, succeeding where the College [of Physicians] has given up in despair, . . . would find ready acceptance . . . in the audiences before whom the play was performed, as consonant with the realities of contemporary life, and not an element of fairy-tale invention."[43] To judge from Harvey's treatment of Sir William Smith for the stone in 1620, for instance, Shakespeare's audience would have seen nothing irregular in Helena's secretly compounding a secret remedy for a large profit. Curious nostrums and books of rare receipts, evidence today of certain quackery, were purchased and used by the fellows of this prestigious College, and though Helena's sex would have prevented her from being admitted to their faculty, women like Frances Worth, a surgeon at St. Bartholomew's Hospital from 1620 to 1650, seem to have been highly respected.[44]

But if such relationships support Helena's disavowal of empiricism, they also glance at a larger medical context Sisson ignores, the dispute between the artists who still followed Galen (c. 130-200) and those who honored Paracelsus (1493-1541). Until the second third of the sixteenth century, neither Galen, the great Greek physician, nor his medieval Arabic interpreter, Avicenna, was seriously challenged, even regarding their fantastic theory of the four "humors." The revolt was begun by Paracelsus, the flamboyant physiologist of Basel, who cast Avicenna's writings into the flames and "inaugurated a new study of pharmacy allied with chemistry."[45] And while Copernicus, Kepler, and Galileo were reordering the heavens, the workings of the human body were closely studied by those who took Paracelsus's cue, among them Vesalius, Servetus, and Harvey. Although by 1600 Galen's authority had been weakened, the notion of the humors persisted well into the seventeenth century and the controversies between the two schools grew increasingly bitter. Granted, those within the same school were not always united: Libavius, a violent anti-Galenist, complained about so many chemists following "the principles and footsteps of the utterly corrupt Paracelsus";[46] Harvey, who is usually associated with the Paracelsian tradition, was by 1613 an officer of the Royal College, a Galenist stronghold; and though Henry IV's personal physician, Theodore de Mayerne, was persecuted by the Faculty of Medicine of Paris for his Paracelsian sympathies, he was later admitted into the English College,[47] perhaps owing to his outspoken Protestantism.

During the plague years of 1603-4, however, the longstanding and usually academic argument took a practical turn and consolidated the ranks.[48] In 1603 Francis Herring, fellow of the College, issued *Certaine Rules for this Time of Pestilentiall Contagion: with a Caveat to those that Wear Impoisoned Amulets as a Preservative from the Plague.* Before the year was out Peter Turner replied with his Paracelsian *Opinion Concerning Amulets or Plague Cakes,* in which he argued that chemicals such as arsenic within the amulets were effective "in all Arsenicall diseases, as the Plague, the Plurisie, . . . Cankers, and Fistulas, and all that kinde." To this Herring retorted as spokesman for the College with *A Modest Defence of the Caveat* (1604), in which he attacks the basic concept of "arsenicall diseases." As a Galenist, Herring was certain that herbal medicines, rightly employed to maintain humoral equilibrium, were the best remedies for all illnesses, not those special chemicals designed to act upon the particular toxicity of a disease. Glancing at Turner's unconvincing explanation of how alchemical distillation could render the noxious effects of arsenic harmless, Herring insisted that "all diseases are cured by their contraries . . . unless you will maintain that dotage of Paracelsus . . . against Galen, that Diseases are cured . . . by their like." Although the schools had quarreled before—in 1602 William Clowes likened their "strife" to what "was in times past betweene Ajax and Ulysses"—the visitation of what the Paracelsians considered one kind of "arsenicall disease" gave special significance to Boccaccio's mention of another.[49]

It would have been uncharacteristic of Shakespeare not to exploit so popular an issue, and Richard K. Stensgaard has recently demonstrated the very probable relationships between the Galenists of the Royal College and the royal physicians whom the King "hath abandon'd" (I. i. 13) as well as between contemporary Paracelsians and Gerard de Narbon, whom the King "would try" since "The rest have worn me out / With several applications" (I. ii. 72-74). The very terms Helena uses to describe her father's prescriptions—"manifest experience," "general sovereignty," "faculties inclusive"—underline several commonplaces of Paracelsian theory as opposed to the Galenist "several applications." While an aura of wonder surrounded the new, strange school, its older, orthodox counterpart enjoyed the support of prestigious learning. Therefore, when Lafew, noting how the King was "relinquish'd of the artists—," is interrupted by Parolles's "So I say, both of Galen and Paracelsus," the audience would have understood the braggart's intrusion as not only impertinent but erroneous, and that Lafew's "Of all the learned and authentic fellows" (viz., only the Galenists) corrects his ignorant coupling.[50]

But why should Shakespeare have taken such trouble to associate his heroine with the unlearned, unauthentic Paracelsian practitioners? Noting that not all empirics were selfish quacks, Stensgaard contends that Helena reminded the audience of those honest, dedicated, unlicensed physicians—"simple, devout folk, pious ministers of the people"[51]—whose freedom to practice was constantly challenged by the learned College. Viewed from this perspective, Lafew's comment on the King's miraculous healing gains some clarity: "They say miracles are past, and we have our philosophical persons, to make modern and familiar, things supernatural and causeless. Hence is it that we make trifles of terrors, ensconcing ourselves into seeming knowledge, when we should submit ourselves to an unknown fear" (II. iii. 1-6). Quite similar are several complaints about the godless naturalism of the Galenist College published by two London divines in 1603 and 1604, the most direct of which is probably Henoch Clapham's warning that "To speak and act in such cases as sole Naturians, is of Christians to become Galenists, and of spirituall to become carnall."[52] And therefore Herring, while attacking Paracelsian cures, also found it necessary to refute religionist views of causes and to defend his colleagues as "Phylosophers" and "learned men."

That Shakespeare wanted us to see Helena's medical rivals as learned, prestigious, and ineffective Galenists is much clearer than that he approved of her own irregular Paracelsianism. If the new school of medicine was "linked with an appeal for religious reform," as Stensgaard argues, and if it attacked the presumptuous Galenist "attempts to explain natural processes not in terms of their divine, inherent infusions but by way of their external, material qualities,"[53] it also had, from the beginning, the vanity and arrogance that often characterize young reformers. What we know of Paracelsus's life, according to one recent historian of science, is "mainly a record or a rumor of his hurried departure from some town or other usually in consequence of the not unreasonable anger of the local authorities—ecclesiastical, academic or medical at some new excess in his ceaseless denunciation of almost every person or opinion held in high regard by the orthodox."[54] In most respects, however, he was as superstitious and error-ridden as his prestigious enemies, offering in place of their unsupported theories "an array of insensible active beings and occult powers . . . whose adoption would have been the strangling at birth of science as we have come to know it."[55] And in place of the authorities he scorned he offered himself: "You men of Montpellier, and Cologne, and Vienna, you Germans, men of the Danube and Rhine, and the Maritime Islands,

Athenians, Greeks, Arabs, and Israelites . . . you shall follow me. . . .
I am to be the monarch."[56]

Such aggressive, pretentious language caught the ear of at least one
Elizabethan, who pictures his "mettle-bruing [i.e., brewing metals
like arsenic and mercury?] Paracelsian, having not past one or two
Probatums for al diseases," making "a pish" at "all receipts and authors
you can name" and being "accounted a Prophet of deepe prescience,"
though but a "mountebanke," a "hungrie druggier, ambitious after
preferment."[57] Two years later the same witty Nashe noted that his
inarticulate opponent was lacking "in the Doctors Paracelsian rope-
rethorique," probably a reference to Paracelsus's middle name,
Bombastes, as McKerrow suggests.[58] Like "empiric" (one who relies
on practical experience, observation, experiment as his sole source of
knowledge *or* a charlatan, an imposter), "Paracelsian" evidently suggested very different meanings, from the humble, devoted, experienced
doer to the vain, ignorant, bombastic pretender. There is, of course,
no question that Helena is a doer, thanks to "the dearest issue of
[Gerard's] practice, / And of his old experience" (II. i. 106-7). But
given her real "motive / For Paris" (I. iii. 230-31), it is difficult to place
her among Stensgaard's "simple, devout folk." In private she has
already listed "The King's disease" as a means to an end, and insisted
that "Our remedies oft in ourselves do lie, / Which we ascribe to
heaven" (I. i. 216-17, 228). Has she changed her mind, or merely her
approach, when she begs the King, "Of heaven, not me, make an
experiment" (II. i. 154)? We shall examine Helena's own "rope-rethor-
ique," along with her tendency to manipulate Providence, in the following chapter. At this point it should suffice to notice that even as she
challenges the Galenists—"But most it is presumption in us when / The
help of heaven we count the act of men"—Shakespeare would remind
us that the Paracelsian habit of counting in reverse was no less
presumptuous.

The third nonliterary context that *All's Well* appeals to is the realm
of politics, especially as it applies to the pursuit of honor military and
civil. The topic is broached in the opening lines of the second scene
with a metaphor hardly heroic: "The Florentines and Senoys are by
th' ears, / Have fought with equal fortune, and continue / A braving
war." Complementing this debasement of warring nations into snarling

curs is old France's illustration of international diplomacy: one word from Cousin Austria, "our dearest friend, / Prejudicates the business" of Florence's request for aid, yet young Frenchmen "who are sick / For breathing and exploit" have free "leave / To stand on either part." As in the cases of wardship and medicine, Shakespeare has accommodated one of his source's relatively minor issues—Boccaccio's Tuscan campaign is merely a convenient activity for Beltramo while self-exiled from Rossiglione—and emphasized its unpleasant aspects.

Would the audience have thought back to another dying king's advice "to busy giddy minds / With foreign quarrels" (*2H4*, IV. v. 213-14)? To use so bitter a struggle as "A nursery to our gentry" certainly resembles Bullingbrook's political opportunism, and we are all the more surprised to hear the King immediately thereafter celebrate Bertram's father as the epitome of old-fashioned integrity (I. ii. 24-48). The King's next long speech on honor (II. i. 1 ff.) is distributed as "warlike principles" which the young Sienese and Florentine volunteers may "Share . . . betwixt" themselves (even, presumably, while they are at one another's throats). In both instances morality first savors of expedience and then turns trite: "Since I nor wax nor honey can bring home, / I quickly were dissolved from my hive" (I. ii. 65-66); "Those girls of Italy, take heed of them" (II. i. 19). That Helena's eventual champion is not pre-eminently qualified to serve as the play's moral spokesman seems even clearer when the French lords "explain" his apparently capricious behavior to the Duke of Florence (III. i.). Since both lords agree that Florence's quarrel seems "holy," the Duke naturally wonders why his "borrowing prayers" have gone unanswered. Their explanation, in effect, is that the ways of the King are, as they have ever been, inscrutable, and that all attempts to fathom them would be futile. "Be it his pleasure," replies the Duke, who evidently appreciates willful authority—his first official act is to promote Boccaccio's hero from captain to "general of our horse" (III. iii.).

We have already noticed how a knowledge of contemporary politics can condition our responses to the play's political events. With the examples of Elizabeth's young favorites before us, for instance, we find Bertram's promotion less improbable. But this does not mean that the original audience found that promotion any less irresponsible than we do. The career of a man like Essex, in fact, made them even more sensitive to the dangers of favoritism. And since it was customary to provide any precocious general with an experienced adviser,[59] they would have noticed even sooner the serious threat posed by Parolles. No part of the political context Shakespeare invokes is as specific as the medical world's Galen or the legal world's wardship, but France's role in the affairs of "higher Italy" must have reminded the audience of that generally intolerable situation which inspired *The Prince*. Before and long after Machiavelli, notes one modern historian, the "wars in Italy provided" not only great booty but "relatively harmless employment for the energies, talents, and rapacity of military aristocracies likely to grow restless or slothful at home where the royal government established and maintained internal order."[60] Nor would a time that had witnessed so many shifts in political and religious alliances have found it difficult to understand Austria's behind-the-scenes maneuvering.

Perhaps the least romantic comment on the pursuit of military honor is one for which an audience of today needs no gloss. The "honors that . . . fly from" the Duke of Florence are largely matters of chance: "You know your places well; / When better fall, for your avails they fell" (III. i. 20-22). But a more important and equally unpleasant reality that the play invokes is for us not so obvious, the sad state to which both civil and military politics had driven the army. Eighteenth-century Englishmen, with the assurances of Marlborough and Blenheim, could freely laugh at Parolles's swagger and Garrick's farce, just as the Victorians could fully enjoy Gilbert and Sullivan's sarcasm about the Queen's apparently bumbling yet actually well-nigh invincible navy. But the original audience's laughter at the military antics of Acts III and IV must have been at times somewhat strained and nervous, for war was never far off and their own defenses were hardly sure. One of England's greatest military historians insists that while Shakespeare satirized "doting justices and rascally captains, . . . he could never have dared to tell even a fraction of the real truth, for the simple reason that England's military condition was in the highest degree dangerous, and that the Queen was responsible for it. . . . To hint at the shameful neglect of . . . Leicester's troops in the Low Countries, or . . . to breathe a whisper to the effect that brave and able soldiers like John Norris trembled over the prospect of the landing of a single regiment of

Spanish regular soldiers . . . would have been perilous to impossibility."[61]

There are nevertheless moments when *All's Well*'s French volunteers seem to have been designed to reflect truths about their English contemporaries that could not be concealed. Leading the list is of course Parolles, "That jack-an-apes with scarfs," that "snipt-taffata fellow" of "scarfs and . . . bannerets" who would even "garter up [his] arms" to reveal that his "soul . . . is in his clothes" (II. iii. 203, 250; II. v. 43-44; III. v. 85; IV. v. 1-2). Officers answering to this description, with a vocabulary to match, could be seen and heard on any street in London, especially during winter-quarters, when recruits were to be raised for the next campaign against the Irish or on behalf of the Protestants in France or the Dutch insurgents in the Low Countries. Poor pay led to desertion and mutiny; low morale allowed commissions to fall to rogues, imposters, and scoundrels "who swindled their men and sent them out to plunder the country for their benefit."[62]

Whether the first Captain Dumain ever went to "Mile-end, to instruct for the doubling of files" (IV. iii. 270), as Parolles alleges, any Londoner could watch such instruction by "experts trained in foreign schools, men who swaggered about in plumed hats . . . swearing strange oaths of mingled blasphemy taught by Spanish Catholics and Lutheran landsknechts, and parting . . . in one long insolent crow of military superiority."[63] And whether the same Captain would actually, as Parolles also alleges, "steal . . . an egg out of a cloister" (IV. iii. 250), such practices were common enough among the Queen's desperately poor troops, victims of her own "imbecile parsimony."[64] "What service canne bee looked for of such soldiers," complained Sir Henry Knyvett in 1596, "as for wante of garmentes and other necessaries ashamed of themselves, perish for could and hide themselves, or Mutenye when they should undertake accions of most moment, And so forced by great extreamities, fall to robbing of theire confederates and frendes, Yea sometymes of theire owne Companions, that most Countries thereby growe wearie of our Nation . . . more then of theire professed enemyes."[65] Finally, there is that unsettling reference to Bertram's "excellent command—to charge in with our horse upon our own wings, and to rend our own soldiers!" (III. vi. 48-50). Actions almost as needlessly destructive can be found among the more theatrical, "chivalric" Elizabethan charges. Zutphen, where Sidney died, was "no more than one of the maddest of the many mad exploits performed by English officers of cavalry," the heroism of an action where "gentlemen threw all discipline to the winds."[66]

But if the Elizabethans found such military parodies too close for complete comfort, they also probably found Parolles's quest for the drum a richer source of comedy than we do. In a world where deeds seldom match words, we relish watching the man who is nothing but talk—and with "a smack of all neighboring languages"—being eventually untongued by "linsey-woolsey," "choughs' language, gabble enough" (IV. i. 11 ff.). Sooner or later we sense that Lafew's question, "is it not a language I speak?" will become some lord's command, "speak what terrible language you will" (II. iii. 189; IV. i. 2-3). Given such careful poetic justice, we are inclined to relegate the drum to a mere pun on "John Drum's entertainment" (III. vi. 38). As "the tongue of war" (*Jn.*, V. ii. 164), however, the drum represented the infantry's sole source of secret yet certain communication. The drummer possessed confidential information and was in battle the center of activity; his special skill in languages helped him to treat with the enemy as well.[67] Relating Parolles's undoing to "this instrument of honor" (III. vi. 66) and trustworthiness is just another example of Shakespeare's enriching his comedy with very general topical meanings.

There is finally Shakespeare's appeal to the world of religion and the play's most specific topical reference, "Saint Jaques le Grand," that famous shrine which Helena, "With sainted vow," promises to visit (III. iv. 7, III. v. 34). Like the dozen editors, translators, and imitators of Boccaccio whom we have already surveyed, Shakespeare has his protagonist feign a pilgrimage in order to accomplish a more wordly quest. But Helena is the only heroine to mention a specific place, and we must again ask whether the playwright, in localizing the story, is not also once more emphasizing its unpleasant aspects.

First, except for G. Lambin's fanciful attempt to identify "great Saint Jaques" as the little-known church of San Giacomo d'Altopascio near Florence,[68] no one has doubted that Helena's alleged goal, however circuitous her route, is the once-renowned cathedral of Santiago de Compostella in northwestern Spain. Its very name (St. James of the Starry Field) witnesses to the legend of those ninth-century hermits in the wilds of Galicia who were led by a great star to the sarcophagus of the Apostle to Spain, the Saint who would soon return to expel the infidels as *Santiago Matamoros,* the "Moor-slayer."[69] Shakespeare's own familiarity with Santiago's special role seems to underlie Iago's indignant "And I—God bless the mark!—his Moorship's ancient" as well as his ominous "Were I the Moor I would not be Iago."[70] Throughout the Middle Ages "pilgrimages to Compostella outshone all others . . . owing to the number of pilgrims of high rank who took part"; from England alone during the Holy Year of 1434 sixty-three ships sailed directly to Spain, while the French became alarmed at the large number of English pilgrims taking the longer route through their country.[71] By the end of the fifteenth century, however, the unbelief that would soon greet St. Thomas of Canterbury was already being expressed by many Christians regarding Santiago. A century before hostile Luther, plain-spoken Langland describes a pilgrim who, for all his scallop shells from Compostella, knows nothing of Saint Truth; a thinner, more ironic smile lies behind Erasmus' portrait of the once-wealthy Saint who now "scarce has a tallow candle" and must offer his pilgrims shells only because "he has plenty of them, the neighbouring sea furnishing him with them"; and in France, of course, the "slim feasting smile of Erasmus became the Gargantuan laughter of Rabelais."[72]

What is most interesting is that throughout the sixteenth century the anger and indignation directed at Santiago come from both within and without the established Church. It is only proper that Sir Francis Drake, having arrived in Galicia in 1589 with an army of 14,000 men, should vow to seize Corunna and destroy Santiago, that center of "pernicious superstition,"[73] or that the Protestant patriot, George Peele, should celebrate this expedition that goes forth "Under the sanguine Crosse, brave Englands badge, / To propagate religious pietie."[74] But Compostella's reputation also suffers at the hands of the loyal Catholic, John Heywood, who includes "Saint James in Gales" among the conquests of his egocentric Palmer, and of the equally loyal Henry Medwall, chaplain to Cardinal Morton, whose rascally low-life characters frequently swear "By Saint James."[75] From the anonymous author of *Frederyke of Jennen* (1518, 1520, 1560), which Shakespeare would soon be using as a source for *Cymbeline,* there are at least two admissions that "God and Oure Ladye" are defending the right, but Santiago is allied with "an olde woman [who] can do that the devell hym selfe can not do," whose pretense for asking the heroine to keep her chest is that "I did vowe a pilgrimage . . . to the holy apostle Saint James, and nowe take I jorney."[76] Small wonder, then, that the anti-Catholic Spenser places in the hand of the arch-hypocrite Archimago "a Jacobs staffe."[77]

Given the frequently hypocritical nature of St. James's pilgrims, it would seem that Shakespeare is once again detailing only to darken. How else do we reconcile the claim of Helena's farewell sonnet, "I am Saint Jaques' pilgrim, thither gone" (III. iv. 4) with her sudden appearance in Florence early in the succeeding scene? Recognizing Dr. Johnson's observation that Florence is "somewhat out of the road from Rousillon to Compostella," G. K. Hunter believes that "it is more probable that Shakespeare would make this mistake than refer to other shrines of merely local celebrity."[78] Hunter is correct that Compostella was well known, but what it was well known for reveals a dramatic theme, not a geographical blunder. How could the playwright who refers to "more lines than is in the new map, with the augmentation of the Indies" (*TN,* iii. ii. 79-80). have proceeded to set north-central Italy between southeastern France and northwestern Spain?[79] Though Florence and Compostella lie in almost exactly opposite directions, the road to Santiago, thematically speaking, leads wherever one's desires dictate. In our concluding chapter we shall see how the paths to Helena's own longings are inevitably paved with religious intentions (or at least religious affirmations). We almost expect eventually to hear how Helena's "holy undertaking[was] with most austere sanctimony . . . accomplish'd," even that "her death . . . was faithfully confirm'd by the rector of the place" (IV. iii. 49 ff.). The play's most specific religious reference is no less discomforting than its appeals to the worlds of law, medicine and politics. What remains is to study the design that renders these unpleasant excursions intelligible.

NOTES

1. *Tudor Drama and Politics,* p. 1.
2. "Shakespeare's Italy," p. 105, n. 1.

3. Bevington, pp. 23, 25.

4. I. iii. 23-24. All citations to Shakespeare are to *The Riverside Shakespeare,* ed. G. Blakemore Evans.

5. See the Arden *All's Well,* ed. and intro. G. K. Hunter, p. 22.

6. *Shakespeare: The Complete Works,* p. 1024. The pamphlet was rpt. with an intro. by A. V. Judges for The Shakespeare Association in 1931.

7. *Shakespeare and the Comedy of Forgiveness,* p. 114.

8. See Hunter, pp. 252-53, n. 10, and Raphael Holinshed, *Holinshed's Chronicles of England, Scotland and Ireland,* I, 527, 531.

9. Robert G. Hunter, p. 114.

10. Ed. Arthur Quiller-Couch and John Dover Wilson, pp. 105-6, 122, 129-30, 137, 169.

11. G. K. Hunter, p. 37; see also p. xxii.

12. Quiller-Couch and Wilson, p. 136.

13. G. K. Hunter, p. 35.

14. "Medicine," in *Shakespeare's England,* I, 433.

15. *Sir John Froissart's Chonicles,* I, 515.

16. Ibid., I, 599. For a modern summary see G. W. Kitchin, *A History of France,* I, 481-85.

17. "The Theme of Ambition in 'All's Well That Ends Well,' " p. 22.

18. Kitchin, I, 460 and Froissart, I, 366.

19. Kitchin, I, 482 and Froissart, I, 583.

20. *Elizabeth I and Her Parliaments: 1584-1601,* p. 91.

21. *An Introduction to the History and Records of the Court of Wards & Liveries,* p. 125.

22. *The Queen's Wards,* esp. pp. 3-10.

23. Ibid., p. 10.

24. Ibid., p. 18. See also Bell, p. 133: "Exploitation by the lessee appeared at its worst where, not content with the income from the ward's lands, he realized a portion of their capital value by selling stock or timber without replacing them, or where, to secure maximum short term profits, he cropped the land till it was exhausted and let farm buildings fall into decay."

25. Hurstfield, pp. 34, 128-29, 142. See also Quiller-Couch and Wilson, p. 172: "The sheriff had charge of idiots whose property was not of sufficient value to make them profitable wards for the Crown."

26. "Wardship in English Drama (1600-50)," p. 478.

27. *The Miseries of Inforst Mariage,* ed. Glenn H. Blayney, 11. 358, 364. All citations are to Blayney's text.

28. Hurstfield, p. 89.

29. Ibid., pp. 140-41.

30. The Countess's uncritical egalitarianism, on the other hand, must have been difficult for the original audience to accept. As we shall see in the concluding chapter, she is unduly impressed by Helena's claims of divine sanction.

31. *Decameron,* ed. Vittore Branca, I, 422.

32. John Florio (?), *The Decameron Containing An hundred pleasant Novels,* fol. T6^V.

33. "The Betrothals of *All's Well That Ends Well,*" p. 183.

34. "Gleanings for the History of a Sentiment: Generositas Virtus, Non Sanguis," p. 102.

35. Hurstfield, p. 139.

36. *The Shoemaker's Holiday,* V. v. 114-15, in *English Drama: 1580-1642,* ed. C. F. Tucker Brooke and Nathaniel Burton Paradise.

37. Ruth Kelso, "Sixteenth Century Definitions of the Gentleman in England," p. 373.

38. Ibid., pp. 374, 382. Kelso is paraphrasing several English and Continental authorities.

39. M. C. Bradbrook, "Virtue is the True Nobility: A Study of the Structure of *All's Well that Ends Well,*" in *Shakespeare: The Comedies,* p. 124.

40. Robert G. Hunter, pp. 117-18.

41. *Eastward Ho,* IV. i. 219, in Brooke and Paradise.

42. Ranald, p. 186. Ranald is paraphrasing Henry Swinburne's *A Treatise of Spousals, or Matrimonial Contracts* (published in London in 1686 but written about 1600), pp. 236-39.

43. P. 20.

44. Ibid., pp. 19-20.

45. J. B. Black, *The Reign of Elizabeth,* p. 312.

46. W. P. D. Wightman, *Science and the Renaissance,* I, 167.

47. Alban H. G. Doran, in *Shakespeare's England,* I, 418-19.

48. The next two paragraphs summarize the findings of Richard K. Stensgaard, "*All's Well That Ends Well* and the Galenico-Paracelsian Controversy," pp. 173-88.

49. Citations from Herring, Turner, and Clowes are found in Stensgaard, pp. 174-76.

50. G. K. Hunter, p. 50, cites John C. Bucknell, *The Medical Knowledge of Shakespeare* (London, 1860), p. 102: "in Shakepseare's time . . . those physicians who would be spoken of as 'our most learned doctors' of 'the congregated college' . . . would not be the disciples 'both of Galen and Paracelsus', but of the former only." Hunter then asks if it is "possible that Parolles is, in consequence, being ridiculed for his fake erudition." Stensgaard, who also cites Bucknill, is confident that Parolles's pretensions to learning are being exposed (p. 180).

51. Stensgaard, p. 183.

52. Clapham's *An Epistle Discoursing upon the Present Pestilence* (London, 1603), sig. A3, is cited by Stensgaard, p. 184.

53. Stensgaard, p. 185.

54. Wightman, I, 246.

55. Ibid., I, 247.

56. Preface to the *Paragranum* (1531), as cited by A. Wolf, *A History of Science, Technology, and Philosophy in the 16th & 17th Centuries,* p. 429.

57. Thomas Nashe, *The Terrors of the Night* (1594), in *The Works of Thomas Nashe,* I, 365-66.

58. *Have With You to Saffron-Waldon* (1596), in *Works,* III, 15; see also Notes, IV, 310.

59. G. B. Harrison, p. 1038.

60. J. H. Hexter and Richard Pipes, *Europe Since 1500,* p. 135.

61. J. W. Fortescue, "The Army: Military Service and Equipment," in *Shakespeare's England,* I, 129.

62. Ibid., I, 121.

63. J. W. Fortescue, *A History of the British Army,* I, 129.

64. Ibid., I, 151.

65. *The Defence of the Realme* (1596), pp. 58-59.

66. Fortescue, *British Army,* I, 148-49.

67. Ibid., p. 153. See also Paul A. Jorgensen, *Shakespeare's Military World,* p. 24.

68. Praz, pp. 96-97.

69. Walter Starkie, *The Road to Santiago,* pp. 1, 21-23.

70. See Geoffrey Bullough, *Narrative and Dramatic Sources of Shakespeare,* VII, 217.

71. Starkie, pp. 66-67. One of the four overland routes, that which crosses the Pyrenees at St. Jean Pied-de-Port, is the road taken by the Countess of Artois, at least as far as Burgos, where she veers south to Valladolid. See *Le Livre du Très Chevalereux Comte d'Artois et de sa Femme,* ed. J. Barrois, pp. 132, 178.

72. Starkie, pp. 50-53.

73. Ibid., p. 58.

74. *A Farewell,* 11. 25-26, in David H. Horne, *The Life and Minor Works of George Peele.*

75. John Heywood, *The Playe Called the Foure PP,* 1. 37, and Henry Medwall, *Fulgens and Lucrece,* Part I, 11. 905, 1119, 1170 and Part II, 1. 108, both in *Five Pre-Shakespearean Comedies,* ed. with intro. by Frederick S. Boas.

76. In Geoffrey Bullough, *Narrative and Dramatic Sources of Shakespeare,* VIII, 68, 71, 76.

77. *The Faerie Queene,* I. vi 35, in *The Complete Poetical Works of Spenser,* ed. R. E. Neil Dodge. See also Dodge's note on this stanza, p. 788.

78. G. K. Hunter, p. 81.

79. The Widow, who hears that Helena is bound for Santiago, promptly guesses that she comes from France and invites her to join other "enjoin'd penitents / . . . / Already at my house" (III. v. 34, 46, 94-96). Her failure to see anything odd about Helena's route could be the result of bad geography on Shakespeare's part. These pilgrims, on the other hand, could be making the rounds, returning from Rome by way of Florence and passing on to Santiago.

VII
Helena and Her Sisters:
A Comparative Reading of
All's Well That Ends Well

> *But now that we have reached this pinnacle, belatedly, it becomes*
> *necessary to make a third examination of earlier scenes* which, in a
> reversal of long habit, the dramatist did not equip us to see in
> their true colours when they were acted. Once more resurveyed,
> the facts of earlier action appear startlingly different: since the end
> of I. i Helena has never faltered in the intents which she then said
> were fixed and would not leave her. She has not made even us
> partners in her enterprise; she has deceived us as she has deceived
> those of her own world. She has long been a masquerader without
> our knowing it. . . . The soliloquy of III. ii and the sonnet-letter
> of III. iv, key statements both, unequivocally announcing her
> purpose to seek the shrine of Saint Jaques and Death, were practices
> upon our own credulity: her pilgrimage was never meant for
> Jaques, but for Priapus.
>
> Bertrand Evans, *Shakespeare's Comedies*

As Bertrand Evans's repeated resurveys indicate, the more
careful our first reading of *All's Well,* the keener our sense that the
desire to know for sure is being frustrated. Until this comedy, Shakespeare's use of "discrepant awarenesses" has always allowed us to know
at least as much as his most knowledgeable characters; we never go
astray if we judge "by the best light the dramatist provided at the
time."[1] In *All's Well,* however, we find ourselves continually forced
to re-evaluate the heroine's words and deeds in the light of later events.
Helena assures us at the close of the first scene that her "intents are
fix'd," for instance, but we are left to guess about their exact nature

until the second act and never realize their intensity until the third. And does not her sudden reappearance in Florence make us anxiously re-examine the preceding scenes, where we though we had "no cause to suspect that [she was] other than an object for pity"? Only at the very end of Act III do we, along with the Widow, finally "see / The bottom of [her] purpose" and thereby "gain . . . the degree of awareness which we gained in *Twelfth Night* in I. ii, and in *As You Like It* in I. iii, when Viola and Rosalind openly announced the beginning of their masquerades."[2] What is even more revealing about *All's Well*, though, is that our second reading proves no less frustrating. We discover that the evidence we must have missed is simply not there, that Helena's decision never again to hinder Bertram's happiness, for example, was made in the sincerity of a soliloquy.

Before concluding that the best light Shakespeare provides in this play was meant only to confuse, we must also remember that the playwright frequently exploited his audience's knowledge of his works' main plots and basic themes. In their first "readings," few Elizabethans would not be watching carefully to see precisely where Richard II's crown becomes Bullingbrook's, when and for what purpose an avenging Hamlet first feigns his inevitable madness, and why important aliens like Touchstone and Jaques have been added to Lodge's popular story of *Rosalynde*. Shakespeare would have been foolish not to take advantage of the spectator's familiarity with his models. In *As You Like It,* Lodge's long-winded exposition is parodied in Orlando's ponderous rehearsal of family history and Charles's report of "the new news at the new court" ("no news at the court, sir, but the old news: that is . . ."; I. i. 96-99). Similarly, in *Twelfth Night* Shakespeare salutes Barnaby Riche's marvelously convenient series of storms and shipwrecks with a breathless volley of chances and perchances (I. ii. 5-8, 21-39). Had the *All's Well* story accrued such sentimental and melodramatic meanings, Shakespeare would have had much the same expectations to take into account. But its tradition had been shaped by the wit and irony of Boccaccio, the cynicism of Accolti, and the nervous expurgations and glosses of Borghini, Salviati, and Painter.[3] There was, in other words, nothing like Lodge's or Riche's romantic exposition, mood, and tone to imitate and outdo. Therefore, if Shakespeare wished to continue paying off each tradition in its own coin, he would have had to reflect the new currency, part of which is the sometimes ambiguous exposition Evans complains about.

It is difficult enough to characterize the average Elizabethan spectator, much less to ascertain his attitude toward a particular narrative. It is very unlikely that even the best informed members of the original audience would have been aware of every treatment we have surveyed. yet the basic meaning of the *All's Well* story, whatever it was, would not have been too complex for the simplest person to grasp, nor would Shakespeare, through his actors' gestures and inflections, have been unable to make that person understand how the old meaning was being elaborated. If the conclusions we have already reached regarding pre-Shakespearean versions of *All's Well* are generally valid, we may assume that the more the audience knew about Helena's sisters, the more suspicious they would be of her own values and motives and even of her self-knowledge. The playwright could encourage or allay such suspicions, but he could never ignore them. The murky exposition we have just noticed suggests a heightening of distrust; so does the unpleasantness of the topical references we examined in the preceding chapter. But only a detailed comparison of *All's Well* to its story will reveal the nature and extent of two crucial relationships: (1) the tradition's influence upon the playwright and (2) the playwright's strategies to influence his audience. Since we are primarily interested in approximating the original audience's dramatic experience—how *they* liked it—we shall examine the first relationship only insofar as it sheds light on the second. Stopping to register every possible borrowing from all probable sources would needlessly burden a scene-by-scene analysis, repeat information at least partly available elsewhere,[4] and complicate an already complex picture.

Although a reasonably knowledgeable Elizabethan would have recognized the outlines of Boccaccio's (or Painter's) story within the play's first one hundred lines—the diseased guardian, the famous physician, the doting girl, the indifferent boy—he must have noticed even sooner that Shakespeare is also bent on recalling his most recent tragedy. Certainly *Hamlet*'s early scenes come to mind when we see the court, dressed "all in black," holding off disease and death with prudent proverbs. Whether Lafew's "Moderate lamentation is the right of the dead, excessive grief the enemy to the living" (11. 55-56) was ultimately inspired by Ecclesasticus xxxviii. 17, 20-22[5] it sounds very much like Claudius's lecture on Hamlet's "mourning duties." Similarly, Polonius's eminently quotable advice to Laertes (I. iii. 58 ff.) seems deliberately echoed in the Countess's sententious blessing upon her own son (we later discover that her chief servant is called Rinaldo). Even as we are adjusting to Boccaccio's plot, in other words, we are also being asked to think of *Hamlet's* situations; no sooner do we notice that two new characters have been added to the old story of ingenious deception than Shakespeare associates them both with Elsinore's most ingenious deceivers. And in the single line spoken by Helena before the stage clears—"I do affect a sorrow indeed, but I have it too"—we find the honest Prince's opposition of appearance and reality merging with Gilettas's indirect designs: Is, madam; nay, it seems, I know not "is."

But if such suspicious associations with *Hamlet* encourage us to continue looking within *All's Well* for its story's traditional mischief, the story's sustained attention to religious rationalizing helps us in turn to notice another relationship between *All's Well* and *Hamlet,* the common theme of shaping divinity. Bertram is no sooner off to Paris with his mother's blessing—"What heaven more will, / That thee may furnish, and my prayers pluck down, / Fall on thy head!" (11. 68-70)—than Helena laments the heavenly order that opposes her love for him, that "bright particular star" so removed from her "sphere." The theme of divine direction is here sounded seriously and sympathetically, as is the Third Day's other motif of sexual desire initiating action: "The hind that would be mated by the lion / Must die for love." It is only at this first soliloquoy's conclusion—"But now he's gone, and my idolatrous fancy / Must sanctify his reliques"—that we catch our first glimpse of the *Decameron's* ironic interplay. For after the conversation Helena engineers with Parolles, where the mask of filial sorrow is exchanged for the mask of witty theorist in the science of virginity, she ceases to be wholly honest with herself and begins translating what heaven seems to oppose into what heaven allows and then into what heaven actively supports. Whether Helen's "idolatrous fancy" recalls that "Mad idolatry" which "make[s] the service greater than the god" (*Tro.,* II, ii. 56-57), her easy, apparently artless transition from sanctifying Bertram's relics to sanctifying her quest for his person brings us back to the naivete of Neifile and her heroine.

Helena's first step in rationalizing her way into Bertram's orbit occurs in her second soliloquy: "Our remedies oft in ourselves do lie, / Which we ascribe to heaven" (11. 216-17). Against the "fated sky" or Fortunes' "mightiest space," the celestial ordering of things she had only moments before subscribed to, Helena now appeals to "nature" or that "power . . . which mounts my love so high." But this is not the vain self-reliance of Cassius or Iago or Edmund, as Helena's detractors sometimes maintain. Interpreting the heroine's guileless self-confidence as "Now, sex, stand up for wenches!" overlooks the naive honesty of her questions, especially the second: "Who ever strove / To show her merit, that did miss her love?" Soliloquies in Shakespeare are sure indications of sincerity. They are not, however, certain signs of truth. If Helena's "remedies . . . in ourselves" is quite different from Iago's "power . . . of . . . our wills" (*Oth.*, I. iii. 325), it is almost as distant from the Christain view of following God's lead, as expressed in the Bishop of Carlisle's "The means that heavens yield must be embrac'd" (*R2*, III. ii. 29). Through his heroine's convenient discovery of the "fated sky['s] / . . . free scope," Shakespeare was not merely relying upon his audience's knowledge of Christian responsibility, as Roland Frye concludes,[6] but also reminding them of the *Decameron*'s irresponsible and sometimes ignorant manipulators of God's will.

Rather than denying Providence, like Shakespeare's villains, or embracing its means, like the reverend Carlisle, Helena quite innocently assumes its role. The process is nearly completed when, immediately after the Countess has sprung her trap, the maid etherealizes that remedy first forbidden and then permitted:

> There's something in't
> More than my father's skill, which was the great'st
> Of his profession, that his good receipt
> Shall for my legacy be sanctified
> By th' luckiests stars in heaven. [I. iii. 242-46]

It is difficult to say whether the "something" supporting Helena's designs relates to Fortune or nature, deity or desire, for throughout this lengthy scene Shakespeare reflects that mingling of the sacred and profane which we encountered in Boccaccio and Accolti. Perceiving that "Her eye is sick on't" (I. iii. 136), the Countess unravels the plot that "only sin / And hellish obstinacy" refused to reveal; Helena eventually admits the "religious . . . error" of her worship, swearing "by grace itself," after the Countess charges her "As heaven shall work in me for thine avail, / To tell me truly" (11. 179 ff.). The Countess's offer to serve as heaven's instrument for Helena's good is especially interesting in view of the maid's own self-appointed role as God's agent in the succeeding scene.

Before Helena reaches Paris, however, both the object and nature of her divine mission receive suspicious glances. We have already noticed the murky politics and trite speeches that Shakespeare invented for the King in I. ii and II. i.[7] He who founds a French nursery upon Tuscan bloodshed, then quickly turns to lecturing Bertram on his "father's moral parts," and at last concludes with a pathetic "I fill a place, I know't" (I. ii. 15 ff.) answers neither morally nor rhetorically to Helena's "One of the greatest in the Christian world" (IV. iv. 2). The heroine's future champion, in short, is a prince whose "dearest friend / Prejudicates" a crucial issue, who resolves the contradictory claims of warring nations by dispatching troops to both sides with a single, all-round call to honor.

But it is the well-intentioned natives of Rossillion who do Helena's cause the most damage. Unlike old France, the Countess realizes that the good old days were not entirely pure: "Even so it [Helena's sickness] was with me when I was young" (I. iii. 128). She is equally convinced, though, that youth often lacks self-knowledge, fails to realize its own defects: "Such were our faults, or then we thought them none" (1. 135). Meanwhile, her Clown follows a less direct course. Just before Helena is forced to admit her "motive / For Paris" and vows that her "receipt / Shall . . . be sanctified," Lavatch comes forth to confess that he is also going a-wooing, claims to be "a prophet," proves that "marriage [and cuckoldry] comes by destiny," identifies Helena with her Trojan namesake, and enforces the sexual motif with his mock-pious observation, "That man should be at woman's command, and yet no hurt done!" (11. 58 ff.). It is in the Clown's whimsical admission of his motives for courting Isbel, however, that Shakespeare comes closest to Boccaccio's theme and tone:

> My poor body, madam, requires it. I am driven on by the flesh,
> and he must needs go that the devil drives.
> *Count.* Is this all your worship's reason?
> *Clo.* Faith, madam, I have other holy reasons, such as they are.
> [I. iii. 28-33]

As the play's "principal exponent of Scriptural quotation,"[8] Lavatch
easily supports his "holy reasons" with several Biblical allusions. For
his ribald puns on holy / "holey and reasons / raisings, however, he
may be indebted to earlier clowns like Boccaccio's Dioneo and Accolti's
Ruffo. The last story of the *Decameron*'s Third Day, after all, treats of
little else than Alibech's holy reasons and Rustico's holy / "holey"
raisings. With probably less knowledge and therefore greater irony, he
who claims to "speak the truth the next way" (11. 58-59) makes us
question Helena's means and ends as effectively as Dioneo glosses
Giletta's. Does this self-proclaimed "prophet" recall Helen of Troy
because he foresees another "fair face" becoming another King's joy,
another "marriage com[ing] by destiny"—Helena's "sanctified" cure—
and another chapter in the history of deeds "fond done"? Does he also
anticipate another "man" soon being at another "woman's command"?
Whether or not it is directed at Helena, his witty complaint against
religious affectation—an "honesty" that "will wear the surplice of
humility over the black gown of a big heart"—certainly gains relevance
as the woman he fetches presently disclaims and then admits "any
token of presumptuous suit" (1. 198).

A similar sexual-religious interplay (with further Trojan associations)
is achieved in the next scene through a more respectable character,
Lafew, who approaches his "royal fox" as "Cressid's uncle" to
announce "Doctor She" and her miraculous powers "to araise" (II, i.
70 ff.). Just as Shakespeare, in the opening scene, used *Hamlet* to help
us understand how he was using Boccaccio, here he recalls a sordid
character from another recent play in order to capture the unintention-
al humor of Neifile's logic and thereby to exploit Boccaccio's joke:
Giletta "begged him as a special favor, to allow her to examine the
source of his disease. She was young and attractive. The King could
not find it in himself to refuse."[9] Giletta, of course, has no one to
usher her into the king's presence; the character closest to Lafew is

Accolti's young gallant, who enters as the flower of courtesy—"servo di donne nato sono"—and departs as the King hints at his former pandering.[10]

Despite Lafew's "light deliverance," promise to "fit" his leige, and identification of himself with Pandarus, Shakespeare resolves the play's first crisis with Boccaccio's mischievous smile, not Accolti's cynical smirk. Granted, critics of the last two generations have worked hard to show that there is no humor of any kind in that curious mixture of miracles, jog trot, and bombast which rises out of Helena's grand confrontation with France. It is an anachronistic sense, they imply, that finds lofty matter deliberately at odds with wretched meter. Tillyard, for instance defends "the pomp and stiffness of [this] rhyme as appropriate to a solemn and hieratic content"; even that tall stuff about "Moist Hesperus" quenching "her sleepy lamp" in "occidental damp," which recalls the rhetorical bravado of *Hamlet*'s Player King, is seen as a serious substitution of "ritual and cloudy incantation" for drama.[11] Noting the Elizabethan dramatists' customary "association of gnomic sentiments with formal couplets," G. K. Hunter, though he finds that elsewhere "satire shadows spirituality," seconds Tillyard's defense: "the verse begins at the point at which a higher note of exaltation is required, just where Helena begins to enforce the claim to divine sanction and encouragement. The dialogue assumes an incantatory, liturgical tone . . . eminently appropriate to the dramatic context."[12]

With the encouragement of *All's Well*'s sources, however, we may find wit qualifying ritual and irony, incantation. We must first notice, though, that many of Shakespeare's gnomic couplets are assigned to his bungling rationalizers, from gaunt Gaunt (*R2*, I. iii. 221 ff.) to vain Vincentio (*MM*, III. ii. 261 ff.). Hunter himself cites *Othello*, I. iii. 199-209, where the Duke of Venice offers Brabantio a series of platitudes in place of his daughter, but whose fine sentiments are upended as the heartbroken father, with heavy sarcasm, pays the Duke back in his own coin. A Shakespearean character apparently earns the right to deliver pointed precepts only through his own present grief or past suffering, like Kent and Cordelia (*Lr.*, I. i. 180 ff.; V. iii. 3 ff.); the sordid maxims of Cressida (*Tro.*, I. ii. 282 ff.) make it clear that the aphorist need not enjoy a sympathetic aura. Had Shakespeare sought to elicit a wholly solemn response to his ostensibly solemn content, he could have easily used the verse and diction of Isabella's moving speech on mercy (*MM,* II. ii. 72 ff.).

In salvaging this scene's comedy, though, we may profit by Hunter's detection of where the "incantation" begins. The first two dozen lines following Lafew's exit flow easily enough: the "receipt" is described, offered, and rejected. Only when the King touches on the supernatural ("to esteem / A senseless help when help past sense we deem," 11. 123-24) does blank verse turn to rhyme and wordplay. Helena next withdraws with mundane sentiments and unrhymed verse, but when France, by way of apology, returns via rhyme to the nearly miraculous ("such thanks I give / As one near death to those that wish him live"), he sets up an eighty-line train of couplets whose allusions range from New Testament proverbs (11. 136-39) and Old Testament exploits (11. 139 ff.) through "The Murther of Gonzago" (which caught the conscience of another king) to the formulaic, fairy-tale request of "What husband in thy power I will command" (1. 194), where Helena first lapses into the familiar form of address.

But the holy maid plays too nicely with her gospel. The sweeping progression inherent in these majestic matters is stifled by such gnomic dainties as "What I can do can do no hurt to try," "But know I think, and think I know most sure," and "Health shall live free, and sickness freely die." The King is given little reason to conclude that "in thee some blessed spirit both speak," least of all in the line immediately preceding: "With vildest torture, let my life be ended" (1. 174). Whether we call this inflated stuff "cloudy incantation" or "priestly puffery," mattter and meter both work toward a high-comic treatment of divine direction, especially after Helena becomes sufficiently inspired to commence rhyming with royalty (11. 147-48) and ironically reverts to her earlier religious rationalizing: "But most it is presumptuous in us when / The help of heaven we count the act of men."

That counting in reverse, no matter how innocently, is no less presumptuous, was a lesson hardly new to the *All's Well* story. Giletta's divine credentials—"Need I remind you that I . . . heal . . . with the help of God?"—are undercut by Rustico's—"he realized that the only way to get to her, was to make her believe she was doing it all in the service of God."[13] Virginia just as frequently deifies her own desires, eventually asking her prince to forgive what was engineered "con pietoso inganno,"[14] And we have already observed how the story's lesson was deliberately blunted by the *Decameron*'s sixteenth-century editors and translators, who either reassign the Third Day's religious rationalizing to the laity or make it less religious in nature.[15]

It is against this tradition that we should understand Helena's "Of heaven, not me, make an experiment." Since the story admits rationalizers of all varieties, from the sincerely misguided to the consciously devious, it is difficult to know whether we should see in its appeal to "heaven, not me" the essence of Paracelsian faith and humility or the height of Paracelsian arrogance, bombast, and hypocrisy.[16] Helena certainly seems sincere when she cites past miracles, and the original audience may have seen in her "great seas have dried" not only a reference to God's parting of the Red Sea, but to its woodcut representation of the title page of the Geneva Bible, above which is printed Moses' promise: "Feare ye not, stand stil, and beholde the salvacion of the Lord, which he wil shewe to you this day."[17]

A misguided sincerity, however, only invites a Dionean perspective. While "greatest grace [is] lending grace," the clown mocks the court the heroine is capturing—his courtly "O Lord, sir!," like the "barber's chair that fits all buttocks" (II. ii. 17), will serve every ass—and then the court mocks itself through Parolles's *and Lafew's* inane dialogue on "a heavenly effect in an earthly actor" (II. iii. 23-24). Like Accotli, whose King exalts Virginia as his "fanciulla pia" and even "per dea l'adora,"[18] Shakespeare plays up Boccaccio's brief notice of the heroine's triumph with religious glosses. But in no instance is spirituality devoid of satire. The "showing of a heavenly effect," after all, is merely "read . . . in what-do-ye-call there," the broadside Lafew is evidently carrying. And just as Parolles seems to be getting the upper hand in the conversation—"he's of a most facinerious spirit that will not acknowledge it to be the—"—Lafew pounces with "Very hand of heaven." "Heaven hath through me restor'd the King to health," proclaims Helena, moments later, as the royal wards are trotted out, and the "youthful parcel" dutifully responds in chorus, "We understand it, and thank heaven for you" (11. 64 ff.).

After Helena has completed her dancing-inventory of the royal stud, Bertram's legitimate objections are not so much answered as blurred with inapposite analogies, sweet sentiments, and open threats. Regal rhetoric notwithstanding, Bertram *is* being brought down. As we have noted,[19] contemporary violations of wards' rights, especially disparagement through enforced marriage, were resented bitterly, and the audience would have quickly spotted the flaw in the King's not-quite-accurate promise to "create the rest." The King cannot create "nobility native," only its inferior, "nobility dative." Nor can he lawfully waive the rights of his less cooperative wards. Even without reference to Elizabethan legal and social documents, though, we should notice that the King's argument on honor severely strains its meaning. If honor without virtue is "dropsied" (1. 128), how can it be "in us to plant thine honor where / We please to have it grow" (11. 156-57)? And if the King repeatedly dissociates honor from that vanity, reputation, in what sense does he use the word in his angry response to Bertram's refusal, "My honor's at the stake"? Instead of representing Shakespeare's views on true honor and nobility, France's arbitrary display of power expands upon Boccaccio's soft-spoken but insistent sovereign in the manner of Accolti's highhanded Alphonso:

> Non è di Regal sangue: Re: è virtuosa.   Prin.
> Nobi[l] non è: Re: ell' è casta, & è bella. Prin.
> Mia casa infamo: Re: tanto è gloriosa.   Prin.
> Che non bisogna aggiunger gloria a quella:
>
>   . . . .
> Principe replicar piu non bisogna
> Ch'ogni tuo replicare è fumo al vento.[20]

Similar measures of wit and irony characterize Shakespeare's handling of the story's second crisis. Feigned or genuine, Helena's humility has hitherto advanced her cause several times. Half suspecting the reason for Helena's sickness but not yet privy to her project, the Countess erroneously believes that "There is more owing her than is paid, and more shall be paid her than she'll demand" (I. iii. 103-05). At a crucial point in her negotiations with France, she momentarily withdraws, "Humbly entreating from your royal thoughts / A modest one, to bear me back again" (II. i. 127-28), but only six lines later she renews her attack with double force. Similarly, it is only after the King has come to regard Bertram's refusal as a personal affront that she resigns her suit—"That you are well restor'd, my lord, I'm glad. / Let the rest go"

(II. iii. 147 48)—a surrender that predictably makes her champion only more militant. Whereas Bertram's father made his inferiors "proud of *his* humility" (I. ii. 44; italics added), Bertram evidently believes that Helena is proud of her own:

> *Hel.*   Sir, I can nothing say,
> But that I am your most obedient servant.
> *Ber.* Come, come, no more of that.
> *Hel.*   And ever shall
> With true observance seek to eke out that
> Wherein toward me my homely stars have fail'd
> To equal my great fortune.
> *Ber.*   Let that go. [II. v. 71-76]

It is difficult to say whether Bertram has really found out Helena in the sense that, moments before, Lafew has "found" Parolles ("When I lose thee again, I care not"; II. iii. 206) or Parolles has "found" the Clown ("Did you find me in yourself, sir . . .?"; II. iv. 33). And it is quite impossible to prove that Bertram's bitterness was influenced by that of Accolti's Salerno, who at this point in the plot rails against the woman who "Ha vinto col suo inganno la mia voglia" (sig. B3ʳ). Beginning with Act III, however, Helena's humble by-paths seem less and less innocent while Shakespeare's likeness to Accolti increases. We have seen that whereas Giletta's shifts take shape slowly and methodically, Accolti startles his audience, using every possible melodramatic device to convince us of Virginia's helplessness before abruptly revealing her strength.[21] Accolti's fondness for juxtaposing sublime pathos with mundane conniving is especially evident when the heroine tells her tearful subjects that she shall spend her last moments wandering in the wilderness, "Poi che non piace al ciel ch'io sia felice," and then admits to her women, some twenty lines later, that "Sol per venir del mio disegno al fine / Celato ho el vero" (sig. C8ʳ-C8ᵛ).

Helena's transition from abject despair to energetic plotting is hardly less startling. In soliloquy she expresses her remorse for chasing her husband from his own country (III. ii. 99 ff.). Equally genuine, it would seem, is her farewell sonnet, in which she vows to do penance for her "Ambitious love" (III. iv. 5). But even here humility is self-enhancing and remorse self-glorifying. To Helena's "He is too good and fair for death and me," the Countess replies, "Ah, what sharp stings are in her mildest words!" More important, the "sainted vow" of "Saint Jaques' pilgrim" to "sanctify" Bertram's name "with zealous fervor" only inspires the Countess to join the King in reverencing Helena's spiritual credentials:

> He cannot thrive,
> Unless her prayers, whom heaven delights to hear
> And loves to grant, reprieve him from the wrath
> Of greatest justice. [III. iv. 26-29]

There are admittedly no clear signs here that the Countess's confidence is misplaced. Only if we have been following Helena's sisters will we quickly sense that such reverence is uncritical and therefore expect the sympathy elicited in this scene to be dispelled in the next.

Although suggestions of highhanded France are found in both the *Decameron* and *Virginia,* Helena's second agent, the Widow, is far closer to Accolti's Costanza than Neifile's "good" and "honest woman," who consistently acts according to her sense of "duty" and "without thought of gain" (pp. 208-10). Whereas Boccaccio could use Dioneo's final story to qualify Neifile's idealism—the Third Day's last word is not the ninth tale's "onestissima" but the tenth's "semplicissima"— Shakespeare, like Accolti, had to establish his counterpoint more quickly. Granted, once Helena has fulfilled the impossible conditions, the Widow seems genuinely convinced of her divine claims:

> Doubt not but heaven
> Hath brought me up to be your daughter's dower,
> As it hath fated her to be my motive
> And helper to a husband. [IV. iv. 18-21]

But the Widow's faith in Helena's authority has been hitherto nourished by something akin to Accolti's "oro," "that which well approves / Y' are great in fortune," the "purse of gold" and offer to "over-pay and pay again" (III. vii. 13 ff.). Surely the specific weight of pounds sterling upon which the good lady is converted to Helena's subtle ethical distinctions is as risible as any of the happier comedies' moral posturings.

> After,
> To marry her, I'll add three thousand crowns
> To what is pass'd already.
> *Wid.*   I have yielded.
> Instruct my daughter how she shall persever,
> That time and place with this deceit so lawful
> May prove coherent. [III. vii. 34-39]

The resemblances between all this and Accolti's moral-commercial dialogues do not establish *Virginia* as one of *All's Well*'s sources; two playwrights fleshing out the same novella may solve their problems similarly yet independently. But even independent similarities can be informative. They tell us that the two dramatists understood the original story in much the same way and, had fortune smiled, would have easily understood one another. Shakespeare's humorous under-scoring of the profit motive certainly seems less cynical and "modern" when we encounter Accolti's monetary references. Though Virginia asks Costanza to second the bed-trick "come el ciel mostra," she first admits to herself that "la forza dell'or troppo è possente."[22] It is Costanza, however, who first skirts the financial issue by decrying materialism, "Chi va a l'util dietro," and Virginia's moralizing over "un si piatoso inganno" is only slightly more religious than the Widow's "deceit so lawful."

Equally informative are the two dramatists' common techniques of underlining the pursuer pursued. Within twenty lines (III. vi. 102-III. vii. 3) Shakespeare has one French lord collecting "twigs" to lime Parolles, another joining Bertram to stalk Diana, and Helena consulting with the Widow to shore up "the grounds I work upon." Helena's own overtures (and the play's three hunts) are of course initiated by Mariana's warning about maidens "lim'd with the twigs that threatens them" and the Widow's casual remark that her daughter might do the Countess "a shrewd turn" (III. v. 24, 68)—valuable information elicited through Helena's by-now-characteristic self-deprecation ("she is too mean / To have her name repeated"). As Helena exits, promising to "bestow some precepts of this virgin," Bertram enters, listening to his lords explain how Parolles can be caught through his own love of "stratagem" (III. v. 100; III. vi. 35). And once the Widow is enabled to see Helena's "purpose" as "lawful" (III. vii. 30), we are prepared for the poetically just deceptions of two deceivers, the wordy captain through his inquisitors' horrendous "linsey-woolsey" (IV. i.) and the ruttish general through one of the best instructed (or at least most preached at) virgins in all of Shakespeare (IV. ii.).

Here there should be no mistaking Shakespeare's method of guilt by association. The woodcock of war yields to the woodcock of love. From the hypocritical soldier's ironic pleas that the very comrades he would betray spare his life, we proceed to the hypocritical lover's resignation of house, honor, and life to his wife's agent, all the while maintaining that his "integrity ne'er knew the crafts / That you do charge *men* with" (IV. ii. 33-34; italics added). Such irony works against the view that the subplot involving Parolles, Shakespeare's largest single structural innovation, was meant to represent the evil that opposes Helena's good within a morality framework. Contributors to the *All's Well* story tend to blur good and evil angels, sometimes mingling grace and vice within a single action (as in Virginia's several "pious deceits") and always portraying life as "a mingled yarn, good and ill together" (IV. iii. 71-72).

It is not the medieval Vice who sheds the clearest light on Parolles's misadventures, but one of his cousins from Roman comedy, Accolti's Ruffo, whom his master soon recognizes as being merely words ("tu pur mi pasci di parole," sig. C3^r) and who condemns himself for fiction-mongering ("Di questo mal n'è causa el frappar mio," sig. B6^r). Like Shakespeare, Accolti keeps his heroine offstage during much of the play's second half, but neither playwright allows us to forget that the humble lady is directing the action, seducing the would-be seducer with plots behind his depth or his designing servant's. "Andiamo," cries Virginia, as she hurries her party to Sabina's inn; "Andiam," echoes the Prince in the very next line, as he hurries Ruffo back to Costanza's house (sig. D1^r). Hardly more than half way though Act IV Ruffo brags about "El fin" revealing his "piu senno fido" (sig. E3^v); about the same point in his play, the knowledgeable Parolles is also "hood-wink'd" (IV. i. 81). But so are their masters. Like Salerno, Rossillion is an amateur Petrarchist and therefore, as he departs, implies that all is well with the most conventional of compliments, "A heaven on earth I have won by wooing thee" (IV. ii. 66). He is already out of earshot, however, when Diana, with a glance at the play's title, accommodates its theme: "For which live long to thank both heaven and me! / You may so in the end."

Nothing in *Virginia* equals the fine irony of Bertram's "heaven on earth," neither Salerno's melodramatic mourning for the loss of a woman he actually shunned (sigs. E1ʳ-E1ᵛ), nor his servant's complaint that women desire only men they cannot have (sig. D1ʳ), nor his chancellors' welcoming speech, "Gratia habbi el ciel, poi che ti ci ha renduto" (sig. E3ᵛ). But just as Costanza'a ambiguous motto—"Et chiede assai chi ben tacendo serve" (sig. D8ʳ)—links Neifile's "onestissima" with one of *All's Well*'s darker corners, so Accolti's subplotting anticipates his fellow dramatist's more successful efforts to enrich a common source. More the parasite than the braggart soldier, Ruffo is crushed with an amorous rather than a military plot: "Quella traditoraccia," Costanza, has flaunted her charms only "per crescere l'appetito" and then "di mercante m'ha fatto l'orecchie" (sig. D7ᵛ). Still, like Parolles, he eventually recognizes and is content to continue living by simply the thing he is: "A me sta ben se ogni vitio osservo, / Che ignobil son plebeo, povero & servo" (sig. E2ʳ). Whether that curious business concerning Parolles's pursuit of Diana for himself (IV. iii. 223 ff.) was suggested by Ruffo's desire for Camilla (sig. B5ᵛ), it is clear that each dramatist designed the servant to embarrass the master, occasionally by direct criticism, more often through similarities in situations or sentiments neither character was entirely aware of.

But it is in *All's Well*'s resolution, the scenes immediately following Parolles's "Who cannot be crush'd with a plot" (IV. iii. 325), that we are most often reminded of Accolti's uneasy balance between high seriousness and high comedy. We have already noticed how theatrically the *secentistico* showman treated the last simple episodes of Neifile's story:[23] her two-line, matter-of-fact explanation of Beltramo's return to Rossiglione is inflated into Salerno's twenty-four-line agonizing, in which ignorance qualifies idealism; her passing reference to Giletta's "many suitors" is turned into Silvio's nine impassioned octaves, where high-flown rhetoric vies with an increasingly exotic geography; her brief notice of Beltramo's "great celebration" becomes fifty-two lines of unrelieved hyperbole, as the Prince's hunters are commanded to bring back a phoenix and his fishermen, several whales and a mermaid; Giletta's straightforward review of the conditions she has fulfilled— less than ten lines of simple prose—inspires Virginia's extravagant summation of her sorrows before the assembled Salernese nobility—139 lines of poetic "ingegno" to make "inganno" look "pietoso" (sigs. E8^r-F2^v); the husband who simply appreciates his wife's "perseverance and wisdom" yields first to a man humbled before heaven's will—"el ciel qui te compiace / Di quel ch'a me non creder gia che annoglia" (sig. F3^v)—and then to a servant-epilogue who insists that all has ended well because "cosi da d'Iddio le giuste voglie" (sig. F4^r).

Although Shakespeare's means are more thematic and structural than rhetorical, his end is finally the same as Accolti's, to achieve the Third Day's ironic interplay within a single plot and thereby convey all the original meanings of the ninth story. Therefore, in the short space between the hero's crushing of his confidant and the heroine's crushing of the hero, Shakespeare first theologizes and then parodies Helena's providential plotting. Finally possessed of ring and child, as well as script and actresses for her grand dénouement, Helena now speaks of "heaven aiding" (IV. iv. 12) with the fullest confidence and consciousness. But no sooner has she insisted that "heaven / Hath brought me up" for Diana's dowry, even "As it hath fated her to be my motive / And helper to a husband" (11. 18-21) than the Clown supplies another theological commentary, Helena as the rueful "herb of grace"— or was it "great Nebuchadnezzar['s] . . . grass"? Lavatch, whose name is, in this context, especially amusing, is evidently once again glancing at the heroine's program. Still "driven on by the flesh," he has renounced marriage and all "Isbels a' th' country" (III. ii. 13, only six lines before Bertram's letter renounces his enforced marriage to Helena) and, consequently, he no longer speaks of "holy reasons." Instead, after Diana has served Helena by pretending to "serve" Bertram—"I think't no sin / To cozen him that would unjustly win" (IV. ii. 18, 75-76)—the Clown must also profess himelf "at a woman's service," for he "would cozen the man of his wife and do his service" (IV. v. 24, 27). Like the *Decameron*'s Third Day, this play features more than one bed-plotter who would serve himself by serving another.

The clearest indication of Shakespeare's closeness to the Dionean

perspective, however, lies in the gratuitous complexities of the final
scene. If Bullough is correct in assuming that the playwright discarded
Giletta'a twins "not only to condense the action but also because they
might seem ridiculous,"[24] a great deal of equally ridiculous scene-
squeezing is still left to explain. Unlike any of her prototypes, Helena
must doubly damn her husband by giving as well as getting a ring, must
employ intermediaries whose theatricalisms recall her own earlier parts
at court, must avoid at any cost confronting her husband (or even her
champion, the King) with the readily available proofs that all conditions have been fulfilled. But why this delight in indirection? Regarded
without reference to her sisters' pious deceits, Helena's manipulations
of truths into illusions and people into puppets have been viewed as
intimations of two of her more powerful though radically different
successors, either the "fantastical Duke of dark corners" (*MM*, IV.
iii. 157), who apparently enjoys an ambush for its own sake, or the
far more sympathetic Prospero, who must proceed obliquely in order
to teach and forgive as well as to chastize his enemies. The *All's Well*
story, on the other hand, encourages us to look for duplicities we may
not be able to prove, a heroine who is a self-deceived deceiver, intriguing
as shrewdly as a ruthless Vincentio while honestly seeing herself as a
benevolent Prospero. From this perspective, the new world at the
play's end is even less brave and new than *The Tempest*'s, and the characters who see anything ending well must share the heroine's naivete.

Long before Helena makes her first feint with the false accusations
of Diana's letter (11. 139 ff.), Shakspeare undercuts the potential
solemnity of Bertram's day of judgment with a series of awkward,
self-conscious moralizings. The strained effect of Helena's maneuvering
through the Capilets, for example, is only anticipated and intensified
by the opening alternations of regal sunlight and thunder, sweet
sentiments for the past and thoroughly pragmatic considerations for
the present. Within the first seventy lines "sweet Helen's knell" is
sounded, silenced, and then rung again as King and court, despite
repeated vows to be "reconcil'd and . . . kill / All repetition," fitfully
contemplate the widower's sins and the bridegroom's virtues. Royal
logic dictates that the circumstances are best remedied by another
march of ward to altar, and Bertram conveniently discovers that it was,

after all, only the beauty of "fair Maudlin" which blinded him to Helena's loveliness. "Well excus'd," returns the King, anxious to patch things up yet unable to resist the inevitable truisms concerning tardy repentance. But when Bertram presents the King's ring as his own "amorous token" for Lafew's daughter, his first lady is again recalled from her grave, thus inspiring a stream of conjectures and evasions which could not have been better designed to facilitate the confusion sought by Helen's gambit. Bertram is hauled off, Diana's charges are read, and while Bertram is being hauled back on to answer them, the King glosses the story's new ring with one of is oldest themes, that of shaping divinity: "The heavens have thought well on thee, Lafew, / To bring forth this discov'ry (11. 150-51).

If the first half of this scene centers in the court's ironic mourning and anxiety over Helena's passing, the irony of the second half is achieved mainly at Bertram's expense. Diana is at her (or Helena's) rhetorical best with some defiant parallelisms (11. 170 ff.), and when her victim lamely retreats to considerations of his "honor," she immediately produces his ring as "a thousand proofs," demanding only hers (actually the King's) in return. Although obviously circumstantial, the incriminating exposition up to this point is, from Bertram's limited perspective, quite factual, and he must escape what he regards as truth with further fictions. What he finally manages, of course, is both a monstrous falsehood and an ironic truth, much like his earlier "heaven on earth." It was Helena, not Diana, who actually "knew her distance, and did angle for me," and it was surely Helena, not her agent, whose "inf'nite cunning, with her modern grace, / Subdued me to her rate" (11. 216-17). While the harried animal is left to "boggle shrewdly," irony is blunted with Parolles's inane equivocations and Diana's series of abusive-playful oracles.

Given the play's frequent minglings of satire and spirituality, however, we should not allow Parolles's wordiness, Diana's incessant riddling or even the exasperated King's angry threats to obscure the haunting significance of Bertram's "modern grace." As applied to Diana, "grace" can only mean "physical attractiveness," a comeliness that Bertram denigrates as commonplace ("modern") and therefore of little importance compared to her infinite or uncommon (cf. Fl's "insuite") cleverness. In the seducer's cruel and subtle attempt to portray himself as the seduced, though, it is just as easy to apply "modern grace" ironically, to Helena, whose allegedly divine shapings have vulgarized God's grace and cheapened His comeliness.

· In the closing moments Shakespeare continues to exploit the court's penchant for muddling through: fair Maudlin is returned to her shelf, Lafew and Parolles are reconciled over a handkerchief, and old France can think of no conclusion more appropriate than risking another enforced marriage by promising Diana the husband of her choice. But the final irony is directed at the heroine. For what purpose all the ingenuity leading to Helena's entrance cue, "one that's dead is quick," and of what worth that which has been "doubly won"? There is nothing to indicate that Bertram's hurried "Both, both! O, pardon!" is any more sincere than his earlier capitulations to majesty ("Pardon, my gracious lord," II. iii. 167; "My high-repented blames, / Dear sovereign, pardon to me," V. iii. 36-37), and it would appear that this third request for forgiveness is also primarily directed at the King: If *she*, my liege, can make me know this clearly, / I'll love *her* dearly, ever, ever dearly" (italics added). To promise eternal love in exchange for a fuller explication may be eminently reasonable, but it is psychologically and emotionally fraudulent. If Shakespeare is attempting to make Bertram's third repentance ring true, he is not working very hard at it. If, on the other hand, the playwright is once again showing us Bertram temporarily bowing to the inevitable, surrendering with a small show of independence, then the hero's last condition is one that he knows the heroine can easily meet. In this case *all*—all that we can see *has ended*—for the time being—*well enough.*

Royalty, however, has the very last words, less confident than heretofore, despite the closed couplet: "All yet *seems* well, and *if* it end so meet, / The bitter past, more welcome is the sweet" (ll. 333-34; italics added). Between the play's title, which claims that all ends well, and its penultimate line, which admits that nothing has yet ended, some confusion there must needs be. The solution is not to glance toward Act VI but to return via an epilogue to the "real" world which has staged this inconclusive piece. Suddenly "the play is done" and the King, now an actor begging for applause, announces that "All is well ended, if this suit be won, / That you express content." The final criterion for all ending well is therefore quite practical: regardless of how the play ends (or nearly ends), all has truly ended well if the audience is pleased.

By this criterion, of course, the play did not end well. It seems never to have been popular, never to have inspired the least contemporary notice, the slightest allusion or quotation.[25] Perhaps some spectators failed to appreciate Shakespeare's witty and ironic application of the Dionean principle. The more perceptive may have resented those moments when *All's Well*'s fooling becomes, like its fool, too "shrewd . . . and . . . unhappy" (IV. v. 63), when it takes on a somberness new to its story. Dioneo, almost always flippant and mocking, never turns bitter or morose. The Count of Artois's darkest deed is attempted with unfeigned love and misdirected idealism. Only Virginia's bleak realization that "io vedo & lodo el meglio, & seguo el peggio" (sig. A3ʳ), a confession Accolti could have found in writers from Euripides and St. Paul to St. Augustine and Petrarch, approximates Shakespeare's unpleasant observations. Lavatch well knows what "wicked creature[s] . . . all flesh and blood are," teaches Parolles to "find me in yourself" and anticipates Edgar's discovery that the prince of darkness is a gentleman (I. iii. 35-36; II. iv. 33; IV. v. 36 ff.). Parolles's inquisitors in IV. iii not only admit the accuracy of his military information—"He's very near the truth in this"—but appear genuinely concerned about his revealing their secrets. Bertram's "A plague upon him! . . . He can say nothing of me" is followed by the first Dumain's indignant "Nay, look not so upon me; we shall hear of your lordship anon" and then by his brother's apparently frightened "Why does he [the Interpreter] ask him of me?" (ll. 116-17, 195-96, 284). Small wonder their earlier agreement that we are "Merely our own traitors" and their later delight in unweaving a web whose yarn is so conspicuously bad; small wonder our own uneasiness when Parolles perceives that whereas no one is plot-proof, only great hearts burst when crushed (ll. 21, 325 ff.).

If these unsentimental pictures of nervous, bitter, selfish and, above all, *little* people were responsible for the play's failure to please, then the Epilogue closes with one final irony. "Ours be your patience then, and yours our parts," pleads the King, hoping to activate the passive spectators. But which of "our parts" would an audience of any time find attractive enough to assume? Faithful to its story's relentless questioning of reasons and rationalizations, *All's Well*'s irony leaves no character untouched, not even the anachronistically egalitarian Countess, whose uncritical acceptance of Helena's religious credentials

(I. iii. 251-56; III. iv. 25 ff.) is no less strange than her failure to answer Helena's greeting at the close. While the play occasionally looks forward to Vincentio's deceptive means or Prospero's charitable ends, it often glances back at young Troilus's relativistic and heavily ironic "What's aught but as 'tis valued?" (II. ii. 52)—Helena as the King's and Countess's "theme of honor and renown" and Bertram as Helena's. More important, how frequently *All's Well*, again like *Troilus*, elicits moral judgments on the bases of moral speeches justifying actions that are at best morally ambiguous.

Read as one chapter of a larger story, however, *All's Well* is no more ambiguous in its tone and mood than *Troilus*. Just as a comparison of *Troilus*'s world to those of earlier versions confirms our sense of Shakespeare's strategies in making "All the argument . . . a whore and a cuckold" (III. iii. 72-73), so our familiarity with *All's Well*'s traditional meanings inspires and supports our treatment of the play as an ironic re-evaluation of shaping divinty. If we do not get its story right, of course, we shall miss much of the play's sophisticated wit and simply conclude that "Shakespeare has taken a fairy-tale and made of it a morality."[26] Granted, the story may ultimately derive from the stuff of fairy tales and folklore, but every medieval and Renaissance handling exploits the ironies of sexual and divine service, even the genteel *Comte d'Artois*. Also granted, this theme of religious rationalization apparently escaped Painter and Borghini, but it clearly amused Boccaccio and Accolti, embarrassed Salviati, and offended Florio. Only the Burgundian chronicler reserves his irony for the hero and his sympathy for the heroine (who reasons skilfully but never rationalizes). And does not Shakespeare's expression of this theme qualify as the "central point of view" G. K. Hunter insists "the play is searching for" and without which parodic scenes "can only have a critical and even disintegrating effect"?[27] If so, we are right in using Dioneo to help us ascertain the relationship between Helena's claims and Lavatch's comments and in employing Ruffo to gloss the similarities between Parolles's experiences and Bertram's.

Above all, this theme makes Bertram's incredible change of heart quite fitting, almost inevitable. To argue that *All's Well* finally fails because its hero's regeneration is unconvincing is to assume that the play was attempting something very different from its story, and to argue that we fail to experience the reality of that regeneration only because we fail to believe in what the Jacobeans clearly saw, "the descent of grace upon a sinning human,"[28] is to forget that we have no trouble believing in Leontes's or Alonso's repentancè and forgivenss. If our hearts are, like Dr. Johnson's, unreconciled to Bertram, it is not because they are anachronistic. It is rather because Shakespeare has measured Helena by her sisters and discovered new ways of capturing the old ironies.

NOTES

1. Bertrand Evans, *Shakespeare's Comedies,* pp. 144, 149.

2. Ibid., pp. 148, 152, 156-57.

3. The only chapter of the *All's Well* story close to Lodge's romance in mood and tone is *Le Chevalereux Comte d'Artois,* with its gentle humor, idealism, and gallantry. Its influence upon any Elizabethan writer is doubtful, however; see Chapter IV, n. 39.

4. The indebtednesses of Shakespeare to Accolti are argued vigorously, if not always persuasively, but two nineteenth-century scholars: J. L. Klein, *Geschichte des Dramas,* IV, 543-90, and Georg Herwegh, ed., *Ende gut, alles gut,* pp. v-xii. The similarities and differences between Shakespeare and Boccaccio are conveniently outlined in Geoffrey Bullough, *Narrative and Dramatic Sources of Shakespeare,* II, 380-86, and in the New Arden edition of *All's Well,* ed. G. K. Hunter, pp. xxvi-xxix. Many of these differences are ambiguous. Does Shakespeare, for example, deprive Helena of Giletta's riches in order to make her pathetic and winsome, as Bullough (II, 381) argues, or to emphasize what Helena herself refers to as "Th' ambition in my love"?

5. Richmond Noble, *Shakespeare's Biblical Knowledge,* pp. 194-95.

6. *Shakespeare and Christian Doctrine,* pp. 162-64.

7. See pp. 104-5.

8. See Noble, pp. 194, 196-97. Of the play's twenty-two quotations, eleven are the Clown's, seven are Helena's, and the remaining four are shared between Parolles (two), the Countess (one), and Lafew (one).

9. *The Decameron of Giovanni Boccaccio,* trans. Frances Winwar, p. 204. Although Winwar's trans. is used throughout this chapter, all citations have been checked against Vittore Branca's two-volume ed.

10. See pp. 59-60.

11. E. M. W. Tillyard, *Shakespeare's Problem Plays,* p. 101.

12. G. K. Hunter, pp. xxi, xliii.

13. Cf. Winwar, p. 213 to Branca, I, 435: "per che s'avvisò come, sotto spezie di servire a Dio, lei dovesse recare a' suoi piaceri."

14. See p. 67.

15. See pp. 77 ff.

16. See pp. 102 ff.

17. *The Geneva Bible* (1560), fol. i^r.

18. See p. 60.

19. See pp. 96 ff.

20. *Verginia* (Venice, 1535), sig. B2^r. The "Prin" opposite l. 3 is obviously a printer's error.

21. See p. 63.

22. See p. 64.

23. See pp. 67 ff.

24. Bullough, II, 381.

25. G. B. Harrison, *Shakespeare: The Complete Works,* p. 1018.

26. Bullough, II, 386.

27. G. K. Hunter, p. xxxv, n. 1.

28. Robert G. Hunter, *Shakespeare and the Comedy of Forgiveness,* p. 131; see also pp. 6-7; 130.

Selective Bibliography

Accolti, Bernardo. *Verginia. Comedia di M. Bernardo Accolti Aretino intitolata la Verginia, con un Capitolo della Madonna, nuovamente corretta, & con somma diligentia ristampata.* Venice: Zoppino, 1535.

Ariosto, Lodovico. *Orlando Furioso.* Ed. Lanfranco Caretti. Milan: Ricciardi, 1954.

Arthos, John, "The Comedy of Generation." *EIC,* 5 (1955), 97-117.

Ascham, Roger. *The Schoolmaster.* Ed. John E. B. Mayor. London: Bell, 1934.

Banfi, Luigi, ed. *Sacre Rappresentazioni del Quattrocento.* Turin: U.T.E.T., 1963.

Barrois, J., ed. *Le Livre du Très Chevalereux Comte d'Artois et de sa Femme.* Paris: Crapelet, 1837.

Bell, H. E. *An Introduction to the History and Records of the Court of Wards & Liveries.* Cambridge: Univ. of Cambridge Press, 1953.

Bevington, David, *Tudor Drama and Politics.* Cambridge: Harvard Univ. Press, 1968.

Black, J. B. *The Reign of Elizabeth.* 2nd ed. Oxford: Oxford Univ. Press, 1959.

Blayney, Glenn H. "Wardship in English Drama (1600-1650)." *SP,* 53 (1956), 470-84.

Boas, F. S., ed. *Five Pre-Shakespearean Comedies.* Oxford: Oxford Univ. Press, 1934.

Boccaccio, Giovanni. *Del Decamerone di M. Giovanni Boccaccio.* Ed. Niccolò Delfino. Venice: Gregori, 1516.

_____. *Il Decamerone.* Ed. Gabriel Giolito. Venice: Giolito, 1546.

_____. *Il Decamerone.* Ed. Girolamo Ruscelli. Venice: Valgrisio, 1552.

_____. *Il Decamerone.* Ed. Guillaume Rouillé. Lyons: Rouillé, 1555.

_____. *Il Decamerone.* Ed. Francesco Alunno. Venice: Gerardo, 1557.

_____. *Le Decameron.* Trans. Antoine le Maçon. Paris: Martin le Jeune, 1559.

_____. *Il Decameron.* Ed.Vincenzo Borghini et al. Florence: Giunti, 1573.

_____. *Il Decameron.* Ed. Lionardo Salviati. Venice: Giunti, 1585.

_____. *The Decameron Containing An Hundred Pleasant Novels.* Trans. John Florio (?). London: Jaggard, 1620.

_____. *The Decameron.* Trans. John Florio (?). Ed. W. E. Henley. Intro. Edward Hutton. London: Nutt, 1909.

_____. *The Decameron of Giovanni Boccaccio.* Trans. Frances Winwar. 1930; rpt. New York: Random House, 1955.

_____. *Decameron.* Ed. Vittore Branca. Florence: Le Monnier, 1951.

Bradbrook, M. C. "Virtue is the True Nobility: A Study of the Structure of *All's Well that Ends Well." RES,* 26 (1950), 289-301. Rpt. in *Shakespeare: The Comedies.* Ed. Kenneth Muir. Englewood Cliffs, N. J.: Prentice-Hall, 1965, pp. 119-32.

Brooke, C. F. Tucker, and Nathaniel Burton Paradise, eds. *English Drama: 1580-1642.* Boston: Heath, 1933.

Brown, Peter M. *Lionardo Salviati: A Critical Biography.* Oxford: Oxford Univ. Press, 1974.

Bullough, Geoffrey, ed. *Narrative and Dramatic Sources of Shakespeare.* 8 vols. London: Routledge, 1957-75.

Calderwood, James L. "The Mingled Yarn of *All's Well." JEGP,* 62 (1963), 61-76.

Calmette, Joseph, *The Golden Age of Burgundy.* Trans. Doreen Weightman. New York: Norton, 1963.

Castiglione, Baldesar. *The Courtier.* Trans. Charles S. Singleton. New York: Anchor, 1959.

Cavalchini, Mariella. "Giletta-Helena: Uno Studio Comparativo." *Italica,* 40 (1963), 320-23.

Chandler, S. Bernard. "Man, Emotion and Intellect in the *Decameron." PQ,* 39 (1960), 400-412.

Chaucer, Geoffrey. *The Workes of our Antient and Learned English Poet, Geffrey Chaucer, newly Printed.* Ed. Thomas Speght. London: Bishop, 1598.

Clubb, Louise George. "Boccaccio and the Boundaries of Love." *Italica,* 37 (1960), 188-95.

Cole, Howard C. *A Quest of Inquirie: Some Contexts of Tudor Literature.* Indianapolis: Bobbs-Merrill, 1973.

Croce, Benedetto. *History of the Kingdom of Naples.* Trans. Frances Frenaye, Chicago: Univ. of Chicago Press, 1970.

D'Ancona, Alessandro. *Origini del Teatro Italiano.* 2 vols. Turin: Loescher, 1891.

_____. *Studi sulla Letteratura Italiana de' Primi Secoli.* Milan: Treves, 1891.

Deligiorgis, Stavros. "Boccaccio and the Greek Romances." *CL,* 19 (1967), 97-113.

De Reumont, Alfred. *The Carafas of Maddaloni: Naples under Spanish Domain.* Trans. anon. London: Bohn, 1854.

De Sanctis, Francesco. *History of Italian Literature.* 2 vols. Trans. Joan Redfern. New York: Harcourt, 1959.

Di Francia, Letterio, ed. *Le Cento Novelle Antiche.* Turin: U.T.E.T., 1930.

Doran, Alban H. G. "Medicine." In *Shakespeare's England.* 2 vols. Ed. C. T. Onions et al. Oxford: Oxford Univ. Press, 1916. I, 413-43.

Doran, Madeleine. *Endeavors of Art: A Study of Form in Elizabethan Drama.* 1954; rpt. Madison: Univ. of Wisconsin Press, 1964.

Dunlop, John Colin. *History of Prose Fiction.* 2 vols. Edinburgh, 1896; rpt. New York: Burt Franklin, 1970.

Evans, Bertrand. *Shakespeare's Comedies.* Oxford: Oxford Univ. Press, 1960.

Farnham, Willard. "England's Discovery of the *Decameron*." *PMLA,* 39 (1924), 123-39.

Fletcher, Jefferson Butler. *Literature of the Italian Renaissance.* New York: Macmillan, 1934.

Florio, John. *Queen Anna's New World of Words.* 1611; rpt. Menston, England: Scolar, 1968.

Fortescue, J. W. *A History of the British Army.* London: Macmillan, 1910.

_____. "The Army: Military Service and Equipment." In *Shakespeare's England.* 2 vols. Ed. C. T. Onions et al. Oxford: Oxford Univ. Press, 1916. I, 112-26.

Froissart, John. *Sir John Froissart's Chronicles.* Trans. John Bourchier, Lord Berners. 2 vols. London: Rivington, 1812.

Frye, Roland M. *Shakespeare and Christian Doctrine.* Princeton: Princeton Univ. Press, 1963.

The Geneva Bible. Intro. Lloyd E. Berry. Geneva, 1560; Madison: Univ. of Wisconsin Press, 1969.

Hexter, J. H., and Richard Pipes. *Europe Since 1500.* New York: Harper, 1971.

Holinshed, Raphael. *Holinshed's Chronicles of England, Scotland and Ireland.* Ed. Henry Ellis. 6 vols. 3rd ed. London: Johnson, 1807-8.

Horne, David H. *The Life and Minor Works of George Peele.* New Haven: Yale Univ. Press, 1952.

Hunter, Robert G. *Shakespeare and the Comedy of Forgiveness.* New York: Columbia Univ. Press, 1965.

Hurstfield, Joel. *The Queen's Wards.* Cambridge: Harvard Univ. Press, 1958.

Jorgensen, Paul A. *Shakespeare's Military World.* Berkeley: Univ. of California Press, 1956.

Kelso, Ruth. "Sixteenth Century Definitions of the Gentleman in England." *JEGP,* 24 (1925), 370-82.

Kennard, Joseph Spencer, *The Italian Theatre.* Vol. I. New York: Rudge, 1932.

Kitchin, G. W. *A History of France.* Oxford: Oxford Univ. Press, 1892. Vol. I.

Klein, J. L. *Geschichte des Dramas.* Vol. IV. Leipzig: Weigel, 1874.

Knight, G. Wilson. *The Sovereign Flower.* New York: Macmillan, 1958.

Knyvett, Henry. *The Defence of the Realme.* Ed. and intro. Charles Hughes. Oxford: Oxford Univ. Press, 1906.

Lazzeri, Corrado. "Arezzo." *Enciclopedia Italiana* (1929).

Landau, Marcus. *Die Quellen des Dekameron.* Stuttgart: Scheible, 1884.

Lawrence, W. W. *Shakespeare's Problem Comedies.* 1931; rpt. New York: Ungar, 1960.

Lee, A. C. *The Decameron: Its Sources and Analogues.* London: Nutt, 1909.

Leech, Clifford. "The Theme of Ambition in 'All's Well That Ends Well.' " *ELH,* 21 (1954), 17-29.

Limoli, Howard. "Boccaccio's Masetto *(Decameron* III, 1) and Andreas Capellanus." *RF,* 77 (1965), 281-92.

Mantovani, Lilia. "Accolti, Bernardo." *Dizionario Biografico Degli Italiani,* I (1960).

Mazzuchelli, Giammaria. *Gli Scrittori D'Italia.* Vol. I. Brescia: Bossini, 1753.

Narducci, Enrico. *Atti della R. Accademia dei Lincei, XII.* Vol. XII. Rome: Salviucci, 1884.

Nashe, Thomas. *The Works of Thomas Nashe.* 5 vols. Ed. Ronald B. McKerrow and F. P. Wilson. Oxford: Blackwell, 1958.

Neale, John. *Elizabeth I and Her Parliaments: 1584-1601.* London, 1958; rpt. New York: Norton, 1966.

Noble, Richmond. *Shakespeare's Biblical Knowledge.* London, 1935; rpt. Folcroft, Pa.: Folcroft, 1969.

Ornstein, Robert, ed. *Discussions of Shakespeare's Problem Comedies.* Boston: Heath, 1961.

Painter, William. *The Palace of Pleasure.* 3 vols. Ed. Joseph Jacobs. London, 1890; rpt. New York: Dover, 1966.

Paris, Gaston. Rev. of "Ueber die altfranzoesische Vorstufe des Shakespeare'schen Lustspiels Ende gut, alles gut," by H. von Hagen. *Romania,* 8 (1879), 636.

Praz, Mario. "Shakespeare's Italy." *ShS,* 7 (1954), 95-106.

Price, Joseph G. *The Unfortunate Comedy.* Toronto: Univ. of Toronto Press, 1968.

Putnam, Ruth. *Charles the Bold.* New York: Putnam, 1908.

Ranald, Margaret. "The Betrothals of *All's Well that Ends Well.*" *HLQ,* 26 (1963), 179-92.

Roeder, Ralph. *The Man of the Renaissance.* 1933; rpt. New York: Meridian, 1958.

Rossi, Vittorio. *Il Quattrocento.* Rev. Aldo Vallone. Milan: Vallardi, 1964.

Santini, Emilio. "Accolti, Bernardo." *Enciclopedia Italiana* (1929).

Scott, Mary Augusta. *Elizabethan Translations from the Italian.* Boston: Houghton Mifflin, 1916.

Shakespeare, William. *Ende gut, alles gut.* Trans. Friedrich Bodenstedt et al. Ed. and intro. Georg Herwegh. Leipzig: Brockhaus, 1871.

——. *All's Well That Ends Well.* Ed. Arthur Quiller-Couch and John Dover Wilson. Cambridge Univ. Press, 1929.

——. *Shakespeare: The Complete Works.* Ed G. B. Harrison. 1948; rpt. New York: Harcourt, 1952.

——. *All's Well That Ends Well.* Ed. and intro. G. K. Hunter. London: Methuen, 1959.

——. *The Riverside Shakespeare.* Ed. G. Blakemore Evans. Boston: Houghton Mifflin, 1974.

Sisson, C. J. "Shakespeare's Helena and Dr. William Harvey." *E&S,* 13 (1960), 1-20.

Smith, G. Gregory, *Elizabethan Critical Essays.* 2 vols. Oxford: Oxford Univ. Press, 1904.

Spenser, Edmund. *The Complete Poetical Works of Spenser.* Ed. R. E. Neil Dodge. Cambridge: Houghton Mifflin, 1936.

Starkie, Walter. *The Road to Santiago.* New York: Dutton, 1957.

Stensgaard, Richard K. "*All's Well That Ends Well* and the Galenico-Paracelsian Controversy." *RQ,* 25 (1972), 173-88.

Tillyard, E. M. W. *Shakespeare's Problem Plays.* London: Chatto, 1950.

Tiraboschi, Girolamo. *Storia della Letteratura Italiana.* 4 vols. Milan: Bettoni, 1833.

Vogt, George. "Gleanings for the History of a Sentiment: Generositas Virtus, Non Sanguis." *JEGP,* 24 (1925), 102-24.

Watson, Curtis Brown. *Shakespeare and the Renaissance Concept of Honor.* Princeton: Princeton Univ. Press, 1960.

Wightman, W. P. D. *Science and the Renaissance.* 2 vols. Edinburgh: Oliver, 1962.

Wilkins, Ernest Hatch. *A History of Italian Literature.* Rev. Thomas G. Bergin. Cambridge: Harvard Univ. Press, 1974.

Wilkins, George. *The Miseries of Inforst Mariage.* Ed. Glenn H. Blayney. Oxford: Oxford University Press, 1964.

Wilson, Harold S. "Dramatic Emphasis in *All's Well That Ends Well.*" *HLQ,* 13 (1950), 222-40.

Wolf, A. *A History of Science, Technology, and Philosophy in the 16th & 17th Centuries.* London: George Allen, 1935.

Wright, Herbert G. "The Indebtedness of Painter's Translations from Boccaccio in 'The Palace of Pleasure' to the French Version of le Maçon." *MLR,* 46 (1951), 431-35.

_____ . *The First English Translation of the 'Decameron'.* Upsala: Lundequistka, 1953.

_____ . "How Did Shakespeare Come to Know the 'Decameron'?" *MLR,* 50 (1955), 45-48.

_____ . *Boccaccio in England from Chaucer to Tennyson.* London: Athlone, 1957.

A Note on the Author

Howard C. Cole is associate professor of English at the University of Illinois at Urbana-Champaign. He is the author of numerous articles and reviews on Shakespeare and Renaissance literature as well as *A Quest of Inquirie: Some Contexts of Tudor Literature* (Bobbs-Merrill, 1973). Professor Cole received his Bachelor of Arts degree from Wheaton College (Illinois) in 1956 and his M.A. and Ph.D. degrees in English from Yale University in 1961 and 1963.